Using Relaxation
for Health and Success

D0892453

Using Relaxation for Health and Success

Stress reducing techniques for confidence and positive health

SALLYANN SHERIDAN
CHRISTINA WAUGH

How To Books

To Mum and Dad, Dinah and Jesse,
with Love and Gratitude

First published in 1999 by
How To Books Ltd., 3 Newtec Place,
Magdalen Road, Oxford OX4 1RE, United Kingdom
Tel: 01865 793806   Fax: 01865 248780
email: info@howtobooks.co.uk
http://www.howtobooks.co.uk

British Library Cataloguing-in-Publication Data
A catalogue record for this book is available from
the British Library

Cartoons by Mike Flanagan
Edited by Barbara Massam
Cover design by Shireen Nathoo Design
Cover image PhotoDisc

Produced for How To Books by Deer Park Productions
Typeset by Euroset, Alresford, Hampshire SO24 9PQ
Printed and bound by Cromwell Press, Trowbridge, Wiltshire

NOTE: The material contained in this book is set out in good
faith for general guidance and no liability can be accepted
for loss or expense incurred as a result of relying in particular
circumstances on statements made in the book. The laws and
regulations are complex and liable to change, and readers should
check the current position with the relevant authorities before
making personal arrangements.

Contents

List of Illustrations

Preface

We all want to be healthy and successful and relaxation plays a vital role in helping us achieve these aims. In this book you'll discover the true benefits of relaxation – how to relieve your mind and body of the impact of internal and external pressures. It will help you recognise if you have too little or too much pressure in your life, and there are checklists to help you assess your current tension levels. There are tips on how to cope with these levels today, but more importantly the book will help you work out longer term plans to de-stress your lifestyle as a whole.

This is necessary because pressure can occur in any area of your life. The relationships you have with others, your sleep and work patterns, and the way you view things, will all have a positive or negative impact on your stress levels. The good things in life can cause additional pressure, too – that long-awaited promotion, an addition to the family, even that well-earned holiday.

Not all pressure is bad. A certain amount of pressure in our lives is healthy – when we combine it with relaxation. And this book shows you how to do just that. By following the relaxation tips, techniques, activities and exercises throughout this book you will become healthier both in mind and body. You will have a more positive, confident outlook, resulting in a happier, healthier and more successful life.

But this can only happen if you *act* upon what you read, and that's often the hardest step. Read the book through once to pick up the overall messages, then read it again, this time absorbing and completing the activities at the end of each chapter. After that, keep it handy to refer to and then live it!

Sallyann Sheridan and Christina Waugh

1

Understanding the Need to Relax

ACKNOWLEDGING PRESSURE

Every day, people the world over experience pressure, whatever their lifestyle. If you work, it's easy to imagine that people who don't work experience less pressure, but that's simply not true. Pressure can occur in all areas of your life including health, finances, home, family, relationships, travel, work and leisure. Pressure can even be imagined. But it's important to recognise that not all pressure is bad. On the contrary, without a certain amount of pressure in your life you wouldn't feel encouraged to try new things, or work on areas of your life that you know need to change.

Pressure bands

If you have too little pressure in your life, you will feel tired and bored and won't have any enthusiasm for the day or the job you're doing. It may take you a day to write a letter that would normally take you five minutes.

When you experience healthy pressure in your life your energy levels rise and you feel challenged and excited by the demands made on you. This is when you deliver your best efforts, feel in complete control and are your most satisfied.

As with so many things in life, however, balance is the key. It doesn't matter how well you're performing, how good you're feeling, you must learn to recognise when enough is enough. Even healthy pressure can escalate into excessive pressure if it goes on for too long or added demands are placed upon you. When this happens you may well end up in an impossible struggle between what you think you can do and what is realistically possible.

If you're thinking, 'This isn't me. I know when I'm doing too much,' don't get complacent. Most people push themselves too hard at some time or another whilst believing they're still managing as well as they've always done.

LABELLING STRESS

Pressure will either lead to growth or stress. So, what is the link between pressure and stress?

Our bodies have a remarkable mechanism known as the fight or flight response. And this response has been with us since the beginning of time. At times of danger your body will produce it automatically without any conscious effort or command from you. This causes actual physical changes in your body which could help save your life if you were involved in an accident, fire or other life threatening incident. It may help you outrun an attacker or carry loved ones to safety from a burning building. It does this by ensuring you have all the energy available in the right areas of your body to defend yourself from a physical threat.

How does the fight or flight response work?

The changes which take place in your body when this response is triggered are instant. The hypothalamus, which is part of your brain, triggers a number of hormonal changes which in turn lead to many other changes occurring in your body, including:

- *Muscles* – tense to prepare for action, and receive more blood to supply energy

- *Heart* – pumps much faster to deliver blood to tense muscles and other relevant parts quickly (your heart rate may increase by as much as 100%)

- *Blood* – pressure rises as a result of the heart's increased activity, and clotting agents are released into the blood to decrease bleeding from wounds

- *Lungs* – breathing becomes faster and shallower to keep up oxygen levels

- *Brain* – more blood flows to it for quicker thinking

- *Digestive system* – shuts down as it's not needed

- *Skin* – blood leaves it to minimise bleeding from wounds and because it's being diverted to muscles

- *Eyes* – pupils eyes dilate to help you see more clearly.

You may be wondering why this should concern you. Isn't it good that your body automatically reacts in this way when you need it? Well, yes ... and no. The fight or flight response is a short-term solution to a physical threat, which was very useful to a caveman fleeing or fighting a sabre-toothed tiger. Today, our pressures are far more likely to be mental and longer lasting:

● being at the end of a long supermarket queue when you're already late

● having a blazing row with your partner because, yet again, they didn't consider your feelings

● being constantly interrupted by people even though you make it clear you're busy.

You know the sorts of things. But the trouble is, whether you're wrestling with a grizzly bear or fuming at being stuck in a traffic jam, your body's response is identical.

If you actually ran away from a burning building, or fought a sabre-toothed tiger, there wouldn't be a problem as you'd burn up all the extra energy your body created. This would lead to a healthy feeling of tiredness which you would relieve by resting. But if you cannot (or do not) burn off the extra energy you keep generating, then you must learn to relax. *Relaxation is the only way you can allow the organs of your body to recover and function normally.*

If you don't relax, your body will go on trying to adapt under increasing strain. It can't. Eventually it will break down and ill health will invade your life. That's why it's vital you learn and use relaxation techniques in all areas of your life. Your well-being depends on it.

So, in answer to the question – what is the link between pressure and stress? – stress is a symptom of the body's inability to cope with *excessive* pressure.

Ignoring stress

Many illnesses are known to be related to stress:

● heart problems

● insomnia

● skin complaints

● bowel disturbances

● muscular aches and pains

● migraines

● high blood pressure

● asthma

● depression

● digestive disorders.

These are just some of the complaints which can be caused by not dealing with stress effectively. After all, we all deal with stress, but some of us choose poor (often destructive) ways to cope – until we know better. And when you consider what happens to your body every time you get wound up it's much easier to understand the direct link between stress and ill health.

It's amazing how many people accept stress-related symptoms as a normal and inevitable part of their everyday life. Perhaps you do? It's not difficult, because stress distorts people's perception so they often don't realise this is happening. But *everyone* has a crisis point, beyond which they can become seriously ill. And by ignoring the signals, they may well suffer one of a number of physical breakdowns including a heart attack, kidney disease or stroke.

So, the more stressed we are or become, the less chance we have of realising it. That's why it's essential to make ourselves aware of the signs.

RECOGNISING TOO LITTLE PRESSURE

Too little pressure can occur when you feel you have no purpose to your life. Someone who is unemployed, retired or in a boring job may find themselves in this situation. People with too little pressure tend to moan about their circumstances, but do little or nothing to change them. They will often be disinterested in other people and their lives and appear disgruntled and irritable. When you suggest ways they could change their circumstances they are unenthusiastic and critical. Even if they do agree to try something different, their courage often fails them at the last and they make excuses and become unreliable. People with too little pressure will often complain of ill health and tiredness

RECOGNISING EXCESSIVE PRESSURE

In common with the above, sufferers of excessive pressure often have low self-esteem. And, as the pressure on them builds, they make poor decisions leading them to become even more critical of themselves. In order to cope with excessive demands, they often work far longer hours than others, but achieve no more. This leads to mood swings and unreasonable and uncooperative behaviour. Ultimately, the person under too much pressure will suffer from anxiety, depression and illness. In severe cases a physical or mental breakdown will be the result.

RECOGNISING HEALTHY PRESSURE

Someone who has healthy pressure in their life

- is cheerful
- feels valued
- is a good planner
- concentrates well
- is concerned about others
- gets on with others
- meets deadlines
- is well motivated
- has plenty of energy
- is cooperative
- is a clear thinker
- has an appropriate sense of humour.

Most importantly, these people are realistic about themselves, their abilities and their limitations. As you can see, people with healthy pressure in their lives are nice to know.

CHECKING YOUR STRESS LEVELS

Take your time to complete the checklists (Figures 1 and 2) which allow you to assess whether you're currently affected by stress – physically and psychologically. Stop reading and complete them now – and answer truthfully!

Now that you have completed both checklists, you can check your stress levels. *Add* the two scores together and compare to the following:

99 and over

Your stress levels are severe and you're approaching burnout. Don't ignore this. Use relaxation and other stress management techniques, although at this stage you may also need to visit your doctor, and/or seek other professional help. Make this a turning point in your life.

Circle which score applies to you:

> **A** = Never
> **B** = Once or less every six months
> **C** = More than once a month
> **D** = Once a week
> **E** = Almost daily

	A	B	C	D	E
Do you feel tight-chested or breathless when not exerting yourself?	0	1	2	3	4
Do you have headaches?	0	1	2	3	4
Does your heart pound for no apparent reason?	0	1	2	3	4
Do you smoke to calm your nerves?	0	1	2	3	4
Do you drink to help you unwind?	0	1	2	3	4
Do you get indigestion/heartburn?	0	1	2	3	4
Do you feel sickly?	0	1	2	3	4
Do you feel unusually tired?	0	1	2	3	4
Do you find it difficult to keep still?	0	1	2	3	4
Do you have unexplained neckache or backache?	0	1	2	3	4
Do you grind your teeth?	0	1	2	3	4
Do you sweat for no apparent reason?	0	1	2	3	4
Do you feel dizzy/light-headed for no apparent reason?	0	1	2	3	4
Do you crave food or nibbles between meals?	0	1	2	3	4
Do you lack appetite at mealtimes?	0	1	2	3	4

Your total score _33_ _15_

Fig. 1. Are you physically affected by stress?

Between 62 and 98
Your stress levels are too high. Take action now or you could put your health at serious risk. Already your body is beginning to adapt to stress, so you must recognise the need to take care of yourself. Use relaxation techniques and other stress management techniques.

Between 40 and 6I
Your stress levels are moderate, but don't get complacent. If you don't practise relaxation and other ways of keeping stress to a minimum, you could find them steadily rising.

Below 40
You appear to be unaffected by stress, which is great. Remember though, like all these scores, they only reflect your current condition. Keep on top of things by practising regular relaxation and stress-busting

Circle which score applies to you:

A = Never
B = Once or less every six months
C = More than once a month
D = Once a week
E = Almost daily

	A	B	C	D	E
Do you find it difficult to choose between things or to make your mind up?	0	1	2	3	4
Do you have sleeping difficulties?	0	1	2	3	4
Do you get irritated?	0	1	2	3	4
Do you lack interest in life?	0	1	2	3	4
Do you find it difficult to concentrate?	0	1	2	3	4
Do you feel angry?	0	1	2	3	4
Do you find yourself rushing from one job to the next?	0	1	2	3	4
Do you find it difficult to relax and switch off?	0	1	2	3	4
Do your thoughts race from one thing to another?	0	1	2	3	4
Do you feel that others have let you down?	0	1	2	3	4
Do you feel isolated with no one to turn to?	0	1	2	3	4
Do you worry about what the future holds for you?	0	1	2	3	4
Do you feel as if you've failed as a parent/child/partner?	0	1	2	3	4
Do you avoid situations/people, rather than face them?	0	1	2	3	4
Do you find it difficult to laugh?	0	1	2	3	4

Your total score _____

Fig. 2. Are you psychologically affected by stress?

techniques – but with a score like this, you probably do that already.

If your score was really low, you may not have enough pressure in your life. In which case, consider taking up a new interest, changing jobs or finding something which will stimulate you physically and psychologically. Use the relaxation techniques outlined in the book to help build your energy levels, and remember, balance is the key.

Whatever your score, *now is the time to take action*.

WELCOMING THE GOOD NEWS
Stress is a serious issue which has major implications on our health and indeed life itself. But many people have come to realise that in removing excessive pressure from their lives they have made exciting positive

changes to their lifestyles. And the self-healing properties of the body mean that by making the changes necessary you can *improve* your overall health, both in mind and body.

Relaxation is vital to this process and in the following chapters you will learn a series of relaxation techniques that will help to improve your overall well-being, your environment, and your lifestyle

COPING IN THE SHORT TERM

There are many different ways in which you can respond positively to situations which cause you pressure. This section looks at things you can do today – in the short term. Coping in the short term is just that, however – coping. It means you are reacting to situations rather than planning longer term stress-proofing techniques.

Here are some short-term coping techniques:

Asking for help
Never be afraid to ask friends, neighbours, support groups, colleagues, even strangers for help. People are often reluctant to *offer* help for fear of being snubbed. So ask! Think of how you would feel if someone asked you for help. You'd give it willingly, wouldn't you?

Delegating
You'll never get anywhere by trying to be everything to everyone. Enlist the help of friends, family, colleagues, whoever it takes. Besides, you'll make them feel useful by getting them involved.

Talking
Problems will not go away because you avoid talking about them. Talking through areas of your life that cause you concern will help bring them into perspective and lead the way to finding a solution.

Taking a break
Take a break from that pile of chores or business reports. This may be something as simple as getting up and walking around the garden, house or car park. You'll return refreshed, less pressured and be far more productive.

Reframing
This simply means looking at the situation in a different way. If you have a disagreement for instance, try viewing it from the other person's angle. It may help you understand why they think as they do.

Removing yourself from the source of pressure
Sometimes, it doesn't matter how reasonable you try to be, the best course of action is to remove yourself from the source of pressure, if only for a minute. It may be a screaming child, an 'I won't take no' for an answer salesman, or an irritating partner. Whoever it is, just do it!

Dropping the shoulders
A lot of tension is held in your neck and shoulders. By deliberately shrugging and dropping your shoulders you can help relieve a lot of that tension.

Thinking a positive thought
Your mind can't think two things at once, so you can choose to oust any negative thought with a positive (possibly funny) one.

Standing back
Sometimes we need to stand back (metaphorically) and look at the wider picture. Ask yourself 'In the great scheme of things does it really matter?' Invariably, the answer is no.

Some of these techniques will be more appropriate for certain situations than others and you need to get used to drawing on one or more of them when a potentially stressful situation arises.

Calming down
Some of the breathing and relaxation skills you'll learn in the next chapter will also be of benefit when you need help in the short term. That's because relaxation is a major key to managing pressure at any time. Mental calm and strength gives you more control over the way you think and act. And, when faced with a potentially stressful situation, it allows you to be aware of all the options open to you. By teaching yourself to remain strong and calm, you will be able to stand back from a situation and come to a more rational decision about your course of action.

You may feel that tranquillity is impossible to achieve when you feel angry, frustrated or afraid. But if you look upon these emotions as a perfectly natural part of life, it will be easier to overcome them. Begin to recognise what causes these feelings and try to express yourself openly wherever you can. In this way you'll start to gain control over your innermost responses, allowing you to act more positively. And you'll find it much easier to feel good about yourself.

PLANNING FOR THE LONGER TERM

Many people shy away from planning things that have no immediate result. They're only interested in a quick fix. But if you're committed to making a difference to your life, you need to accept that some things take a little longer. The good news is, the sooner you start, the sooner you'll start getting the results you want.

We use the term 'stress-proofing' our lives, but in truth, that's simply not possible. All of us at some time in our lives will be affected by events that are seemingly out of our control such as redundancy, floods, disability, maybe even the death of someone close to us. In view of this, your aim should be to reduce stress or minimise its effects where possible. And to increase your resistance – which brings us back to planning.

Taking action

There are certain areas of your life which you need to examine. Areas which, when you start to change them, one by one if necessary, will make a real difference to the way pressure affects you now and the way it will affect you in the future. It makes sense to look at, and, where necessary, improve your:

● communication skills

● level of physical fitness

● eating habits

● sleeping patterns

● attitude

● relationships

● home environment

● job and working habits

● interests

● relaxation skills and techniques.

Throughout this book we will be looking more closely at all these areas to help you focus your efforts in the right direction. The positive effects of doing so may be experienced quite quickly in some instances. Others will take longer, but you can rest assured that you will be putting building blocks into place that will have a positive impact on your life in the coming months and years.

ACKNOWLEDGING THE NEED FOR CHANGE

Nothing stays the same, as much as we would sometimes like it to. Change is inevitable. As it's happening anyway, why not assume it's for the better? The thought of redundancy or early retirement often fills people with dread. What will happen to them? In reality, many people have used this situation to bring about a change in their lifestyle they'd previously only dreamed about. Using their redundancy or their new free time, they turn their lives around

Jim, who was made redundant from an engineering firm after 25 years' service, took the opportunity to change career completely. He now builds and sells rustic garden furniture. Jim openly admits that he would never have taken the plunge whilst he still had a 'secure' job. But now he earns a good living doing what he enjoys most – and he's never been happier.

Jim's story isn't unique. Millions of people now look back on an event they'd initially dreaded and cite it as a positive turning point in their lives. These include divorce, redundancy, retirement, disablement, unemployment, returning to college, moving home, and changing career.

CASE STUDY

David recognises he has to make changes

David's working longer hours than ever, but achieving less and less. Some of his colleagues have been made redundant and he's worried he'll be next. He hardly spends any time at home and when he does he and his partner usually end up rowing and she accuses him of being unreasonable. David feels he's let her and their children down, but he can't seem to switch his mind off work. Because he's having trouble sleeping, David starts drinking more than usual before bedtime, thinking it will help. After weeks of feeling unwell, he eventually visits his local medical centre. The doctor prescribes tablets and warns David that unless he slows up and takes life a bit easier, his high (and rising) blood pressure will cause him real problems. David recognises that sooner rather than later he must make changes.

KEY POINTS

- The fight or flight response is the same whether you're faced with a major or a minor challenge.

- The fight or flight response is the same whether you're faced with a physical or a mental threat.

- When faced with a stressful situation, you must either use up the energy created by the response or learn how to turn it off using a conscious relaxation technique.

- It is healthy to have a certain amount of pressure in your life.

- There are several techniques that you can use to help you cope with increased stress in the short term.

- Long-term planning will help you reduce stress permanently.

ACTIVITY

You know that a certain amount of pressure can help you feel fulfilled and valued. Think back to a time when you felt this way. Perhaps you:

- clinched a lucrative business deal

- helped a neighbour out of a crisis

- received praise for a job well done

- met the challenge of hosting unexpected guests.

Remember how good you felt? Close your eyes for a few minutes and recreate those warm feelings of self-worth.

2

Learning How to Relax

The fact that we have to learn how to relax says a lot about our modern way of life. But it is essential if we are to counteract the effects of the physical and psychological strain we live and work under.

The opposite of the fight or flight response (outlined in the previous chapter) is the relaxation response which arises from our being fully relaxed. This response allows our internal organs to work more efficiently and has a beneficial effect on our blood pressure, digestion, heart and breathing rate, and a whole host of other biochemical functions. It has a positive effect on our mind and moods too.

As enjoyable as watching your favourite soap on television can be, it's not relaxation. Relaxation is a series of progressive exercises through which you systematically empty your mind and muscles of stimuli and tension.

RELAXING AS A PRIORITY

To gain the most from relaxation you need to make it a priority in your life – not something you do when you remember or when you find yourself with time on your hands. People who do make relaxation a regular part of their everyday lives, say they:

● have more energy

● feel calmer

● make better decisions

● do not get irritated or angered so easily

● enjoy a better sense of overall well-being,

and it has a positive effect on their emotions. It's easy to see, therefore, why people who do practise regular relaxation make it a priority.

On a practical note, relaxation has no harmful side effects and essentially costs you nothing to practise. All you need is yourself and a little time.

If you truly want to relax, you'll always make time and space available. People who cannot find a quiet space in their homes often drive to a quiet spot to practise, or do so late at night or very early in the morning. Be determined to reduce your stress levels and improve your life, then you'll find a way.

BREATHING TO HELP YOU RELAX

Before we learn some relaxation techniques we need to examine another very important part of our everyday lives – the way we breathe. Every day we can take as many as 20,000 breaths, sometimes more. Mostly we are not aware of the fact as our attention is focused elsewhere. We can consciously control our breathing, however, by making it faster or slower, deeper or shallower.

You know that when you get stressed your breathing quickens, and when you are relaxed your breathing is slow, deep and rhythmic. Therefore, taking control of your breathing is an essential part of learning to relax. And in doing so you will exert a positive influence on your physical and emotional well-being.

Breathing test

Before you start any of the exercises in this book, try the following breathing test, standing, if you can. And remember, unless you have blocked nostrils, all breathing should be through the nose.

1. Put one hand flat on the upper part of your chest.

2. Put the other hand on your stomach, just below your rib cage.

3. Breathe as normal, noting which hand rises first at the start of each breath.

Did your upper or lower hand rise first? If your lower hand rises first then you are breathing correctly. If the upper hand rises first, your breathing is inefficient as you are not using your lungs to their full capacity. Therefore you need to take more breaths per minute, which means that other parts of your body have to work harder too. Practise breathing consciously until your stomach rises first.

Many of us breathe incorrectly at some time, when we are anxious, tense or feeling scared, for example. But if you notice that you frequently breathe incorrectly you need to address this.

Overbreathing

Overbreathing is essential sometimes. When you run or exercise hard, your body needs to keep up oxygen levels. And if you suddenly face a crisis, it's appropriate for your body to trigger the fight or flight response. But if you find yourself overbreathing (hyperventilating) without any real need, breathing and relaxation techniques help. Not only do we overbreathe when we are anxious, faulty breathing can also *cause* symptoms of anxiety which in turn will make your breathing worse. It's a vicious circle, and people who overbreathe on a regular basis often have many other symptoms such as palpitations and dizzy spells.

Try the following test

1. Sit in front of a mirror in which you can see your upper body.

2. When you are comfortable and relaxed, take a deep breath.

3. As you breathe in notice what happens to your shoulders.

Do your shoulders rise towards your ears? If so, it's likely you are overbreathing on a regular basis, although if you have a respiratory problem, such as asthma, this can be common.

If you do overbreathe habitually, consult your doctor for advice and try breathing and relaxation exercises.

RELAXING 'ON THE GO'

There are times when you'll need a quick relaxation technique, such as when you are finding a situation or someone particularly stressful:

● before a difficult meeting with your bank manager

● before an important interview with a prospective employer

● when you're having a disagreement with a friend, neighbour or partner

● when speaking in public

● when you have to make a complaint

● when you're faced with queues and delays and you're already late.

Typically, in these sorts of situation, you may have a physical response, with your heart beating faster, your breathing shallow and rapid, your palms sweaty and your mouth dry.

Practise this:

1. Shrug your shoulders several times before dropping them.

2. Make yourself aware of your pulse and your breathing.

3. Relax your jaw, letting your lips part slightly.

4. Breathe in through your nose.

5. Breathe out (loudly and explosively if possible; if not, just say 'let go' to yourself as you do it).

6. Do this a few more times. then breathe more slowly and deeply.

7. Smile.

What's great about this technique is that it can be done anywhere – at work, in the car, at a relative's house, in a supermarket queue – without anyone even knowing you're doing it! A quick and easy way to relieve sudden 'nerves' and tension.

ADOPTING THE RIGHT POSTURE

We are often completely unaware of the tension we hold in our bodies. And unless we get rid of the tension using relaxation techniques we find ourselves suffering from backaches, headaches and a whole lot of other tension-related problems.

Drop your shoulders now – how far have they dropped? And what about your hands where you're gripping this book? Try holding it loosely. If you're unsure of where you're holding tension, tense a muscle first, let go and notice the difference. Get used to checking all your muscles this way to see where you're regularly holding unnecessary tension.

Shallow breathing can also be a sign of bad posture, which in turn puts extra strain on other bodily organs. That's because each action in one area of our body impacts on another, which is why it's essential to try and work on your whole body.

Of the many stresses and strains poor posture puts on the body, the most common is back pain. The following exercise is one which will help you stretch your back. It is not a relaxation technique, but one of many exercises you can do to stretch and tone your back. It will also work on your hips and the backs of your legs. If you have an injury or other physical restriction never attempt this or any other exercise without first consulting your doctor. Practise the following slowly.

Stretching the back

1. Sit upright on the floor with your legs stretched out in front of you.

2. Keeping your back straight and your feet pointed up towards the ceiling, stretch your arms out straight in front of you.

3. Keeping your feet in the same position, lean over your legs towards your feet, and grip them if possible.

4. Straighten up again.

5. Again stretch your arms out towards your feet to grip them, but this time point your toes away from you.

Repeat ten times.

POSITIONING YOURSELF TO RELAX

Using breathing and the quick-fix relaxation technique mentioned above is great for those times when you are suddenly faced with a stressful situation. But when you come to practise regular relaxation techniques it's best to make a little more preparation. You need to be warm to relax, as your muscles will automatically contract (tense) when cold, and wear loose clothing when possible. Try to make the room or area free of noise and interruptions, and as tranquil as possible. Then adopt whichever position is most comfortable for you:

Sitting
If you choose to sit when relaxing, sit with your back straight, place your hands loosely in your lap and both feet flat on the floor.

Standing
If you prefer to stand, put your feet in a position that's comfortable for you, and round your shoulders forward allowing your arms to hang loosely in front of your body. Keeping your back straight, let your head fall forward so your chin rests on your chest.

Lying on your back
Lie flat on your back on a firm bed or on the floor, with a flat pillow

beneath your head. Your arms should be alongside your body with your palms facing upwards. Try and keep your legs reasonably straight, with your feet slightly apart. Have your heels facing each other with the toes of each foot facing away from the other. But you must be comfortable, so place other pillows where you need them – under your knees, for example.

Lying on your front
Lie face down on the floor or on a firm bed with your head turned to one side. Rest your cheek on the floor on whichever side you find most comfortable. Lay your arms alongside your body with your palms facing upwards. Keeps your legs fairly straight with your heels apart and toes facing towards each other.

Kneeling
Kneel on the floor (or mat) with your knees together and your toes pointing out behind you. Bend over so your forehead is resting on the floor slightly in front of your knees. As you do this lower your backside towards your heels. Place your arms alongside your legs so that your hands, with palms facing upwards, are beside your feet. Round your shoulders loosely.

USING DEEP RELAXATION TECHNIQUES

One of the easiest ways initially to enter a state of deep relaxation is to purchase a deep relaxation audio tape. Many such tapes are available. The authors of this book have produced one, details of which are in the Useful Addresses section at the end of the book. Alternatively you may wish to record the following deep relaxation exercise onto a cassette yourself. You can use a tape at a time which suits you, in the privacy of your own home, or wherever you choose to play it. *When entering a state of deep relaxation you must never be doing anything which needs your concentration, such as driving a car or operating machinery.*

Deep relaxation exercise
Before starting this exercise, make yourself comfortable and close your eyes. Take several deep breaths, exhaling slowly every time, and concentrate on those parts of your body as they're mentioned.

... Now that you are feeling warm and comfortable, take a deep breath, filling your lungs, and let your breath out slowly (pause) ... take another really deep breath, filling your lungs again, and this time breathe out slowly (pause) ... take another deep breath, fill your lungs completely and then hold your breath for as long as you feel comfortable (pause) ... now let your breath out slowly and already you can feel your body starting to relax ...

Now let this warm feeling of relaxation drift all the way down your body to your feet (pause) ... your feet are very warm, very comfortable and very relaxed (pause) ... now this warm flow is moving from your feet to your ankles ... now it's moving up your legs into your knees ... you feel so relaxed ... this warmth flows from your knees into your thighs ... from your thighs into your hips ... from your hips into your stomach, and with every breath you let go you feel your whole body releasing tension and becoming more and more relaxed ...

Now allow this warm relaxed feeling to flow up your back ... it's now flowing up into your shoulders and down into your chest ... it's a wonderful feeling ... and with every breath you let out you become more and more relaxed ... feel the warmth and relaxation move down your arms to your elbows ... from your elbows to your wrists ... from your wrists into your hands (pause) ... feel all tension leaving your body through your fingertips ... you feel so relaxed, so comfortable ...

Now the warm relaxing flow moves up into your neck ... now up into the back of your head ... over your head and down into your forehead ... all your brow muscles are relaxing ... your eyes are relaxing ... the muscles around your eyes are relaxing ... you feel your cheeks relaxing ... now your chin ... allow your jaw to drop so you have no tension left anywhere in your face (pause) ... you feel so warm, so comfortable, so very relaxed ...

All your muscles are free of tension, and the longer this relaxation continues the better you feel, and the better you feel, the more your body relaxes. So relax and let yourself go ... relax and let yourself go ...

You are becoming even more relaxed (pause) ... every part of your body is relaxing ... every tissue, every organ, every gland is relaxing ... making you feel so relaxed and content ... so just relax and let yourself go ...

The deeper into relaxation you go, the better you feel ... and the better you feel, the more your body will relax. You are feeling better, happier and contented (pause) ... you're feeling positive and confident ... and as each day passes this confidence and contentment will grow (pause) ... your ability to make good decisions is growing ... you are choosing to view the positive aspects of all situations (pause) ...

At night when you go to bed ... you will sleep soundly ... each and every night (pause) ... you will drift into a deep sound sleep which is so restful that nothing will disturb you ... unless an emergency occurs ...

then you'll be wide awake, physically and mentally alert and able to deal with the emergency in a calm and resourceful way (pause) ... when the emergency passes you will return to bed and drift back into a deep sleep ...

In the mornings you wake at the time you wish ... you feel refreshed and alert (pause) ... you feel happy and content (pause) ... notice how all discomfort has left your body ... and how resourceful you feel (pause) ... notice the way you feel now ... supple, healthy, resourceful, confident, motivated, optimistic, happy and content (pause) ...

Now as you open your eyes, take a minute to adjust and remember the wonderful relaxed way you feel right now (pause) ... these empowering feelings will stay with you (pause) ... you will sleep well, be healthy and live happily.

Brain activity
Your brain emits four types of waves which vary according to your state:

● Beta – this is your normal conscious rhythm

● Alpha – when you are deeply relaxed, tranquil but awake

● Theta – a sleepy, dreamlike state

● Delta – when you sleep and dream

Using biofeedback equipment, health professionals can measure brain wave activity, and relaxation is shown to bring about alpha and theta rhythms.

Meditating
Meditation is a skill which you learn and get better at with practice. it allows you to focus on the moment and is an effective way to escape the pressures and stress of everyday living. There are many different ways of meditating, Buddhist and transcendental meditation methods being but two.

During meditation your breathing and heart rate will slow. And your brain wave frequency changes to alpha waves, which, as described above are a sign of deep relaxation. It's easy to see then why meditation is so beneficial in helping people on their way to overall wellness. Meditation has also been shown to relieve many undesirable physical and psychological states, such as anxiety, sleeplessness and panic attacks. To gain most from meditation you need to practise it for at least 20 minutes every day.

Simple meditation

1. Ensure the room or area is warm and quiet.

2. Sit on a cushion on the floor and make yourself comfortable (use a chair if you're unable to do this).

3. Close your eyes lightly, drop your shoulders, and release your body of tension.

4. Breathe in rhythmically, making full use of your lungs' capacity.

5. Focus your attention on one positive word you've chosen (such as love, peace).

6. Continue to breathe rhythmically, repeatedly focusing on your chosen word.

7. Do this for 20 minutes and then sit quietly for a few minutes

8. Stretch your arms, legs, neck and stand up

Repeat this daily.

If your mind wanders
Every time you find your mind wandering, accept the fact, let the thought pass through and return to your original positive word. With practice you'll soon be able to spend at least 20 minutes of every day focusing totally on the here and now. Bliss!

If you wish to explore ways of meditating, you can join classes or contact meditation centres. With transcendental meditation you will be given your own word in Sanskrit, and encouraged to meditate twice a day for 20 minutes each time. But there's nothing to stop you developing your own methods or a mix of techniques. Another joy of meditating is that it helps you get things into perspective.

DEVELOPING YOUR RELAXATION SKILLS

You will naturally find ways of developing your own relaxation skills. This may mean changing the way you've always done things. If you're one of these people who always has to answer the phone – unplug it before you start relaxing. Consider joining a weekly relaxation class, stress management course, or one of the many one-day workshops run by colleges. Or how about visiting a retreat for a day or two to unwind completely? This needn't be costly. Some Buddhist monasteries run a programme of guided meditation retreats which are suitable for beginners.

Above all, make time for yourself

Tips to help you relax

- Find a quiet place where you won't be disturbed.

- Make your setting tranquil.

- Keep your eyes lightly closed.

- Ensure you are warm.

- Breathe through your nose unless otherwise stated.

- Do not chew gum or anything else during relaxation.

- Do not imagine yourself engaging in anything physical.

- Get into the habit of listening to relaxing music.

- Wear loose clothing.

- Care enough about yourself to practise relaxation at least twice daily (three times would be even better) for at least 15 minutes each time.

CASE STUDY

Claire protests about her lack of personal space

Claire's A-levels are looming and she feels extremely tense and snappy. She has read about relaxation and its many benefits, but she finds practising it difficult. With five younger brothers and sisters, finding a quiet spot where she won't be interrupted seems impossible. Music is always coming from one of the bedrooms and the TV in the sitting room is seemingly on permanently. Following a row with her parents about her lack of personal space, Claire's mother comes up with an idea which won't upset any of the other children. Clearing the junk from an outside shed, she installs a portable heater and a floor mat. Now every evening, Claire goes into the shed with a personal stereo and relaxation cassette and practises deep relaxation for at least half an hour.

KEY POINTS

- To gain the most from relaxation you need to make it a priority in your life.

- Taking control of your breathing is an essential part of learning to relax.

- Relaxation has no harmful side effects and costs nothing to practise.

- Relaxation brings about biochemical changes which also help induce feelings of tranquillity and happiness.

- You can also use relaxation 'on the go' to help you meet particularly stressful situations.

ACTIVITY

Stop! Without altering your posture or your breathing take note.

- Are you breathing correctly?

- Are you holding tension in your body? Your shoulders, perhaps? Your hands? Your jaw?

Now begin to breathe more slowly and deeply and relax these areas one at a time.

By scanning your body for tension like this every so often, you'll soon discover where you tension spots are.

3

Developing Other Ways to Relax

Setting aside time which is just for you is therapeutic. Combining it with relaxation, massage, or an aromatherapy session can make it heavenly. Why not develop your own relaxation strategy and make it a regular part of your life? The immediate benefits are that you will be more relaxed and calm, and in the long term you will notice an improvement in your overall well-being and ability to enjoy life.

So, what other methods can you use? There are many, and this chapter will outline some of the more popular ones. It's worth remembering that you are unique, however, and methods which work best for someone else many not work best for you. Try as many of the alternatives as you can and see which you enjoy most.

USING VISUALISATION

Visualisation is such a powerful tool that it is being used increasingly in business and education. Writers and artists use it to aid creativity, health professionals use it to help treat anxiety and combat stress, and trainers use it to boost self-esteem and confidence. People from all walks of life now use visualisation both at home and at work – with great success.

As with relaxation, it's best to find somewhere quiet and free from interruption while using visualisation techniques.

Visualising the outcome you want
You're going to visit someone you normally find difficult. A belligerent relative or a demanding client, perhaps. Make yourself comfortable, relaxed and close your eyes. Now imagine yourself arriving and the person greeting you. Make the vision as realistic as possible by smelling the smells there – coffee, perfume, or new carpets. What can you see – a stone cottage, or an office door? Feel the ground beneath your feet – is it grass, carpet, tiles? Hear the sounds – are there people tapping on computers, birds singing, or a radio playing? Make it as real as you can. What colour is the cottage door? Is the office door glass or wood? Is there a name or number on it? Smile warmly at the person and notice how pleased they are to see you. You see a genuine smile spread across

their face as they welcome you. They invite you into their office or home and offer you refreshment and ask how you are. They are as truly happy to see you as you are to see them. Notice how much more relaxed you feel. All past friction has dissolved and a new understanding has taken its place.

By replaying this scene over and over in your mind you are helping to change your perception of the event. As a result your behaviour will change too. Now when you arrive at your relative's or client's, you will act differently, which will result in them doing so too.

Visualising the life you want

How often have you moaned about being overweight, not having enough money, or your nose being too large? These problems are often compounded by the way you talk to yourself. If you avoid looking at yourself in the mirror each morning and say 'I'll always be fat. I'll never lose weight', then, guess what – you probably never will. Those negative thoughts will become so implanted in your subconscious that you will only ever act in a way that reinforces them.

Change the way you talk to yourself and the images you have of yourself. Visualise walking into a clothes' shop and choosing the clothes you'd love to fit into. Feel and smell the fabric of the suit you've chosen. Look at the label – it's the exact size you want to be. Notice how easily you slip into the suit. It fits perfectly. You see yourself in the mirror, the ideal weight you wish to be, in the clothes you like to wear. You look sensational. The assistant compliments you on the way you look. Repeat this over and over.

Don't generalise

Remember to be specific when visualising. If you'd like a different job, visualise yourself in the one you want. Does it involve working in a team or working for yourself? Visualise yourself going to that job, wearing the appropriate clothes and receiving your first pay cheque. See your name on the cheque, the figures showing how much you've earned, and the name of the bank on which it's drawn. Isn't it a great feeling? Practise this technique with all areas of your life.

As with all life-enhancing exercises, visualisation needs to be practised regularly to help you become who and what you want to be.

TAKING UP YOGA

Yoga literally means union, to bring together. Essentially, it is a way of life. This way of life would be extremely difficult in our modern Western culture, but we can use it to benefit the way we think, act and feel. By learning the correct way to breathe, stretch and relax, yoga dramatically improves our overall physical and mental health.

One of the joys of yoga is that you can take it up at any age. The postures you need to adopt are practised slowly without jerking or pushing, so you cannot strain your body or injure yourself. And the postures can be adapted if you have a physical problem.

By gently stretching all parts of the body, yoga also massages internal organs and glands. And by combining this stretching with yogic breathing you will relax your mind and body and stimulate your circulation. Yoga is great, too, for reversing the stiffness associated with tiredness and ageing.

All over the country, yoga classes are run in schools, colleges and private venues. Many people start learning about yogic postures and breathing this way, under the guidance of a qualified yoga teacher. Or you can choose to have individual sessions to explore more advanced postures and techniques. There is also a wide range of books and videos available to help you get started.

One way that you can start to help yourself today is by practising the following breathing exercise:

Alternate nostril breathing exercise

1. Sit comfortably with your back straight.

2. Close your eyes and breathe in and out through your nose.

3. Breathe in again through your nose, then close your right nostril with your right thumb and breathe out fully through your left nostril.

4. Pause and inhale through your left nostril to a count of two.

5. Using your fingers to block your left nostril as well, hold the breath and count to eight.

6. Release your thumb and breathe out fully through your right nostril, pause and count to four.

7. Keeping your left nostril closed, breathe in through the right nostril to a count of two.

8. Close both nostrils and count to eight.

9. Release your left nostril, and breathe out to a count of four.

This counts as one round. With practice you'll soon be able to do ten rounds daily.

Don't cheat. You must breathe out slowly all the time you are counting – do not breathe out fully and simply stop taking another breathe until the correct number is reached!

With further practice you can increase to the ideal ratio of breathing in for four, holding for 16, and breathing out for eight. But don't be concerned at how long it takes to achieve this, it may well take weeks of practice.

INTRODUCING YOURSELF TO AROMATHERAPY

Aromatherapy is therapy (massage) using aroma (essential oils). Its aim is not to treat disease but to bring about a greater sense of physical, mental, spiritual and emotional well-being. This is achieved by inhaling essential oils or by massaging them into the skin. Essential oils are obtained from a wide variety of flowers, plants and trees and, depending upon which you choose, will either stimulate, soothe or heal. Lavender is good for relieving stress and anxiety for example, but remember to check the oils before using as some (such as lavender, rosemary, marjoram) are unsuitable for pregnant women.

Inhaling oils

When essential oils are inhaled they act on your brain and nervous system and, depending on the oils you've chosen, will either help to dispel fatigue, encourage concentration or ease depression. They can be inhaled straight from the bottle, or you can place a few drops on a tissue and breathe in the fragrance for a few seconds. If you're feeling tense, try this with a few drops of a relaxing oil, such as lavender or jasmine. A couple of drops of lavender on your pillow at night will aid sleep, but be careful not to let any undiluted oils get onto your skin as they may produce an allergic reaction.

Another way to inhale essential oils is by placing them in a burner, which you can buy from a health or gift shop. Burning oils in this way allows their essence to pervade the air, which in turn has a profound effect on your mood. Another excellent way to inhale essential oils is to use them in a bath, allowing their fragrance to be released through the steam. Or, if you have a cold, you can add camphor, eucalyptus or peppermint oil to a bowl of hot water – 10 drops for every 100ml hot water – and inhale the vapour by leaning carefully over the bowl and covering your head with a towel.

Bathing to unwind

● Run a warm bath, adding six drops of lavender oil and four drops of geranium oil as the water's running *or* seven drops of sandalwood oil and three drops of marjoram oil.

● Climb in and enjoy this truly unwinding experience.

● When you get out of the bath, rub a pre-prepared mix of oils into your skin using slow rhythmic movements. (This could be six drops of camomile and two drops of rose oil added to 20ml of pure grapeseed oil).

Massaging oils

Before applying to the skin, essential oils must be mixed with a carrier oil such as pure grapeseed or almond oil. Two drops of essential oils to every 5ml of carrier oil is the recommended mix. Massaging these oils into the skin is the way they are most commonly used. In addition to the wonderful effects brought about by massage, the oils are partly absorbed through the skin where their powerful constituents are released into the tissues and bloodstream. You can massage the oils into certain parts of your own body such as hands, face and front of the body, but there is nothing quite like a session with a qualified aromatherapist.

Choosing and storing essentiai oils

You must choose oils which are 100% pure, as these will be free of chemical additives and artificial fragrances. You need to store these in a cool dark place, such as a sealed box in an unheated room. Prices do vary but the purest oils are more expensive as they are more costly to produce. The uses of aromatherapy are many, and there are books available which will help you decide which oils are for use in certain conditions. As a general guide:

● lavender and geranium help you unwind

● camphor, hyssop or lavender applied on a compress help relieve bruising

● sandalwood, sage, rose, marjoram, cypress and clary help sleeplessness and irritability

● basil and rosemary are stimulating.

Many qualified aromatherapists also sell essential oils, and will be happy to recommend which ones you should use. Certain oils, such as basil and rosemary can aid concentration for example, so are useful if you or your children are studying, or if you have reports to write.

DISCOVERING THE JOYS OF MASSAGE

The beneficial effects of massage on our minds and bodies has been understood for many thousands of years. The stroking, kneading and rubbing movements help relax tense muscles. When massage is given by a qualified practitioner, it improves circulation of the blood and has a positive impact on the nervous system, heart and other organs of the body. It can also help to reduce pain in arthritic conditions, hasten healing and improve people's moods. Its aim is to ease away tension and to restore unbalanced energy, but it also works to help prevent future weaknesses in the body.

Massage is a shared experience. The person receiving the massage must trust the giver if they are to relax fully. It's vital, too, for the giver to be relaxed and have empathy for the person they are massaging. If you have ever been given a massage by a qualified masseuse, you will know just how beneficial and therapeutic it can be. Commonly, tension is found in the neck, back and shoulders. Tense muscles feel hard and knotted, whilst relaxed muscles are firm yet flexible, a bit like putty.

Preparing to massage your partner

Make the room warm and conducive to relaxation. Have your partner lie on their front, either on a couch or on the floor. This must be at a height which suits you, as any discomfort you experience when massaging will be transmitted to your partner. If your partner lies on the floor, place a mattress or folded blanket beneath them and kneel at their head facing down their spine. Try to make your movements flowing and smooth, keeping your hands in contact with your partner's body all the time.

1. Relax for a few minutes before giving a massage.

2. Put the massage oil into your warm hands to allow the oil to warm.

3. Put your hands gently on your partner's upper back.

4. Move your hands slowly down either side of the spine.

5. Once you reach the buttocks move your hands outwards and pull them up the sides of your partner's back before sweeping in across the shoulders to meet at the upper back again.

6. Repeat this rhythmically to ensure the back is well oiled.

7. Constantly check with your partner that you're using the correct pressure.

Now you need to move to the side of your partner and concentrate on those areas where the muscles feel knotty. There is likely to be tension in the shoulder blades, so place one hand under your partner's shoulder and use the fingers of your other hand to work in pressing circular movements around the top of the shoulder. Then work around the shoulder blade. Finish the massage by repeating steps 3 to 7 above.

You may like to suggest your partner drinks plenty of water following a massage as this helps flush toxins from the system.

Other forms of massage

There are many different types of massage, Tai, Indian, and Swedish, with practitioners specialising in all the various methods. Indian head massage, for example, involves massaging the face, scalp, neck and shoulders without oils or creams, and is said to be a great stress buster.

Self-massage can also be done on many areas of your body including your hands, head and feet. Massage your temples for two minutes with your fingertips. The gentle strokes you use will reinforce the need to be kind to yourself

MAKING YOUR MIND WORK *FOR* YOU

The way you think could well determine how long you live. Research shows that people who are optimistic and think positively live longer. They're also healthier than pessimists. It makes sense therefore to become an optimist – if you're not already. We've all heard people say, 'But that's just the way I am', or, 'I'm too old to change'. But you'll be pleased to know that's simply not true. People can change – providing they have a good enough reason to do so.

Worrying

How much time do you spend worrying? Is your job secure? Is your partner faithful? Will you pass your exams? Will your children get into trouble? Does your daughter's husband treat her fairly? Will you end up alone? Can you make the mortgage this month?

Worry takes the place of activity. By making yourself act instead of worrying you can really start to get a grip on your problems. If you're worried about getting a job – act. Prepare a CV, ring companies, write letters, tell people you know and meet that you're seeking work, study more, keep presentable, remain optimistic, visualise yourself getting the job you want. Do, do, do! You'll go to bed much happier every night knowing you've done everything you possibly can to maximise your chances.

Many people don't take action because they're afraid of failing or making fools of themselves. Therefore, they do nothing and end up worrying about things instead. If you don't call that company about the job you want, you can't make a fool of yourself can you? But then neither can you get the job. The only way you'll get better at taking action is to practise. Visualise yourself calling the company and getting the result you want – then do it.

There are, of course, things you can't do anything about, or so it seems. Perhaps you're worried about your daughter's unhappy marriage. You can't make decisions or choices for her. All you can do is be a good example by making the best of your own life and by offering a happy supportive environment for her to visit. Besides, are you sure you're not 'worrying' about someone else's problems to avoid having to deal with your own?

Self-talk

You choose the words you think and say, and mostly they're habits. Start getting into new habits today by consciously choosing to think positively:

- say *challenge* instead of *problem*

- and start saying *I choose to ...* instead of *I ought to ...* or *I should ...*

- say, *I will remember* not *I'm bound to forget*

- and before an important interview or meeting, say *I am very calm and resourceful* not *I'm really nervous.*

Now you're aware of it, you'll be amazed at how many negative phrases and words you use when speaking to yourself. You'll notice how habitually negative others can be too. So the next time someone asks you what the weather's like outside, don't say, 'it's lousy', say, 'it's raining'.

LOOKING AT OTHER WAYS TO RELAX

When exploring all the possibilities, remember it's important to find methods which suit your individual needs best. Follow your intuition about the practitioner too. You may find you enjoy massage, but you can't seem to develop a rapport with the practitioner. Shop around, as it's important to find someone with whom you can be open and comfortable.

Reflexology
Reflex points on our feet correspond to different parts of our bodies. Practitioners gauge which parts of your body are affected and work on the appropriate points to treat and help prevent mental, physical and emotional problems.

Bach Flower Remedies
Dr Bach created a completely natural system of healing by transferring the potency of wild flowers into pure spring water. These remedies are used to improve emotional well-being and come ready-prepared in health shops and chemists. By far the most famous of these is the Rescue Remedy, which is a combination of five Bach Flower Remedies – rock rose impatiens, clematis, star of Bethlehem and cherry plum. It's used to help people cope with stressful situations such as taking an exam, speaking in public, receiving bad news or having problems with friends or family. If you feel unable to choose which of the remedies (or which combinations) to use you may consider contacting a practitioner. The Dr Edward Bach Centre (details in Useful Addresses) holds a register of practitioners and other general information.

Zero balancing
Stretching and pressure is used to balance energy and help relieve tension which builds up deep in the body's structures. A state is arrived at within the body where mind and body balance in harmony, creating a smoother, more relaxed demeanour. After initial treatments (which vary in number according to the individual condition) some people use this combination of body work and healing every few months as a maintenance programme.

Homeopathy
Homeopathy is an alternative form of medicine, based on the theory that 'like cures like'. In other words, ailments are treated with small doses of drugs that in a healthy person would produce symptoms like those of the illness. As the *person* is treated as opposed to the condition, if two people have the same symptoms they may not necessarily be treated with the same substances.

Alternative therapies

There are numerous other methods you can explore including Shiatsu, Reiki, cranio-sacral osteopathy, Alexander Technique, acupuncture and herbalism. Only you will know which is right for you. Consider also contacting a stress management consultant. These are trained professionals who specialise in supporting people, whilst guiding them towards solutions.

CASE STUDIES

Steve finds it difficult to relax

After being pressurised by his partner to take a week's holiday with their young children, Steve finally agreed. For the first few days he was unable to relax at all and snapped at everyone. His partner urged him to take advantage of the aromatherapy treatment offered at the hotel and reluctantly he agreed. Despite his initial scepticism, he was pleasantly surprised to feel more relaxed afterwards. So much so, he had an aromatherapy massage every day for the rest of the holiday, and encouraged his partner to do the same while he looked after the children.

Helen is forced to seek advice

One evening when Helen told her husband how miserable her life was, he snapped. Said he was sick and tired of hearing her moan about everything – the weather, the neighbours, her life, when she never did anything about it. They went to bed not speaking. The next day he came home from work and said he'd booked her an appointment with a stress consultant. Despite her initial fury, Helen went – her husband had never had such an outburst before. She was heartened to find that the consultant understood how unfulfilled she felt, unlike her family. As a result, she felt more positive and looked forward to the appointment she'd booked herself for the following week

KEY POINTS

- Massage, aromatherapy and yoga are examples of alternative therapies which promote wellness and can be used as part of an overall relaxation strategy.

- Positive thinkers are healthier than negative thinkers.

- Visualisation techniques help change your perception and, consequently, your behaviour.

- Explore all the possibilities to find methods which suit your individual needs best.

- Remember that to get the best results it is important to find a practitioner with whom you can develop a rapport.

ACTIVITY

You know positive thinking is beneficial. It also helps to repeat statements (affirmations) which are positive, personal, and in the present. Examples could be:

- I am a successful person/writer/singer/parent – put whatever you wish to be.

- I love who I am and everyone in my life.

- Every day I am wiser, happier and healthier.

Now make up some of your own if you wish. Say them to yourself repeatedly and write them down over and over again. Notice how much better you feel when you say positive things to yourself.

4

Finding Time to Relax

Time. Everyone wants more. Time to write letters, time to have coffee with friends or heart-to-hearts with family and loved ones. Time to take a breather, go to places you've always wanted to visit, clear out the garage, speak with your boss. Time to pursue your own interests, sort through years of old photographs, or time to just sit and do nothing.

Time is elusive. Every day you start out with hours and hours before you. If you work, study, have family, a partner or children, a large part of the day can be dominated by other people. Even if it isn't, how much of any day do you really have for yourself?

BALANCING YOUR LIFESTYLE

Balance is the key to so many aspects of our lives, and so it is with managing time. When we are under pressure it is easy to lose sight of what's really important; and when we have too little pressure we often procrastinate and achieve little. Everyone has to spend a certain amount of time eating and sleeping, and in many cases working too. But it is often the time outside of these areas which causes us the most problems.

Family and friends
The size of your family and the number of friends you have will often determine how much time you can spend with them individually. It will also affect the amount of time you spend alone. If you're in a relationship, you must also spend time together; just the two of you. This is not an indulgence; it's an important step in keeping a relationship alive and healthy.

Spending time alone
If you're constantly surrounded by other people either at work or at home, you must make space for yourself. Spending time alone with your own thoughts, relaxing, making lists or writing up your journal is a necessary part of everyday life. Never believe this is a waste of time.

Nor is sitting idly, watching the world go by. Or engaging in a pastime which you enjoy. It helps your overall contentment levels and allows you to become more productive in all other areas of your life.

ORGANISING YOUR TIME

We live in a world that's more time-conscious than ever before. We are surrounded by time-saving gadgets – automatic washing machines which can wash and dry our clothes while we sleep, computers, fast cars, planes and trains, microwaves, pre-chopped and pre-cooked foods, fast-food outlets – yet most of us still say there are not enough hours in a day. Why? Because most people do not organise their time efficiently.

Have you ever wondered how some people manage to fit so much into their lives? They work, relax, meet friends, have hobbies, attend evening classes, write books, enjoy holidays and help out at charitable events. They often have partners and families too. The answer is they organise their time well. And the key to that is planning.

Writing a blueprint

Do you take each day as it comes? Moaning when it doesn't go how you'd like and feeling lucky when it does? If you want to build a life that's fulfilling and rewarding, a certain amount of pre-planning is necessary. Don't just drift, become the architect of your own life. And when you've decided what you want it to hold for you, commit it to paper, a sort of 'blueprint' if you like. Be specific, too. It's no good saying, 'I want to be rich', that's far too general. But if you say, 'I'd like to own Coastguard's Cottage outright in three year's time', then you've got a tangible target, something definite to aim for.

Your aim may be to have an equal loving relationship. Write down the tangible aspects. What character traits do you seek in this partner? Humility, compassion, sense of humour, integrity? Pick up a pen and paper now and write down your main goal(s). Write a time limit alongside, as in this example:

Own Coastguard's Cottage outright	3 years
Spend more time with Linda	3 months
Be able to run five miles	9 months
Start saving £20 a week	Now!

Checking resources

Now examine and write down the resources you need to achieve your aims. Be realistic. For example, if you've an arrogant streak and like nothing better than a good gossip it's unlikely you'd attract someone with humility and integrity!

Once you've identified what you've already got and what you need to obtain your goal(s), you can set about closing the gap. To own Coastguard's Cottage, staying with our example, you may need a better paid job, or to buy and renovate a house which you can sell at a profit, or perhaps you could start expanding a part-time business venture. These are just three possibilities. If you're a smoker who wants to save £20 a week and be fit enough to run five miles – quit smoking!

Scheduling

Now you know what you need to do, you have to work out the steps to reach your goal. If, for instance, you've decided you want a better paid job, you may need additional qualifications. Find out what qualifications you'll need, how long they'll take to obtain and enrol in the class. Do this with every aspect of your blueprint. You then need to incorporate these steps into your everyday life plan – and stick to them!

WRITING LISTS

Making lists is an essential ingredient of a well-planned life. These may appear time consuming at the outset, but once established they take little time to update and your reward is a fulfilling productive life. Not just for you, but for everyone around you. You'll find yourself doing more, having more free time, and feeling less stressed. Besides, there's something quite magical about committing tasks, ideas, plans and dreams to paper. It seems that the very act of writing them down reinforces your commitment to making them happen.

Remember it is equally important to schedule your leisure time too. Put aside time to enjoy days and evenings out with your children, partners, friends and family.

Layering your plans

Initially you need to layer your plans. Start with a yearly schedule, transfer this to a monthly view, followed by a weekly plan, then daily lists.

Most importantly

Whilst you have a full 365 days laid out before you, put a large tick through a few days and evenings of your choice. The more the better. These are days that may seem a long time ahead, but are to be set aside for *you*. They're for you to do as you want with. This could be your chance to indulge or pamper yourself; take a nostalgic day trip, laze in a sunny field, or visit a gallery or exhibition.

Yearly schedule

Look at your long-term schedule and see what you want to do and by when. Imagine you've decided that a City & Guild's qualification will give you the better paid job to help purchase Coastguard's Cottage (using our example). The classes run for two hours every Wednesday evening at the local college for the next 12 months, plus two hours a week for homework. Plot these five hours a week on your schedule. Five hours because you need to allow an hour's travelling time to and from college.

Don't forget!
Now plot onto your schedule the days you'd like to spend with others. Perhaps your parents have a special anniversary coming up – block the day off if you want to spend it with them. By planning this far ahead you can ensure nothing thwarts your good intentions when their special day comes around. Write in family and friends' birthdays, graduation ceremonies, any celebration or time together you wouldn't want to miss.

Monthly schedule

Your monthly schedule is an expanded version of your yearly one. It carries greater detail and becomes more definite. If you are going to a ruby wedding celebration at the end of June, for example, you may want to start looking for a suitable present a month beforehand. If so, make a note to do so in your May schedule.

Weekly plan

On your weekly plan write in times against each 'activity', like this:

<u>Wednesday 12 September</u>

6.30 a.m.	Relaxation	6.30 p.m.	College
9.00 a.m.	Work	10.00 p.m.	Write diary/lists
5–6 p.m.	Cook/Eat	11.00 p.m.	Relaxation

Daily lists

Every evening spend a few minutes making a <u>To Do</u> list for the following day. Be thorough and include things such as:

A   book car in for MOT
B   ring doctor for appointment
A   leave spare key in outhouse for Mum
A   take pitta bread out of freezer
A   collect coat from dry cleaners
C   finish letter to Irene
B   return library books
A   hand in Personnel Report
A   buy drinks/nibbles for evening guests
C   buy new coat

Prioritising

Once you have completed your list, set about prioritising. As shown above, the most common way of doing this is by putting an A against activities which are essential (such as 'hand in Personnel Report'); a B against important things you'd like to get done, but which are not essential (such as 'return library books'); and a C against things you'd like to do once the more important A and B issues are dealt with. Once you've prioritised in this way, make time for these activities in your day. And always allow more time than you think you need.

So often we end up doing 'urgent' things and never get around to doing the important things we really want to. Beware of allowing C activities (such as writing letters to friends) to get constantly pushed onto the following day. If you notice this happening, give them a higher priority – and hey presto, you'll make time to do them!

Ticking off

Carry your list with you – in your wallet, bag, car or pocket. As you complete the tasks on your list – tick them off or cross them through. It feels good to see the items being dealt with one by one and it encourages you to move on to the next task. You can always put some really basic things on your list, such as 'getting up' or 'having breakfast'. This way you start the day well, having already completed a couple of activities!

MAKING TIME FOR DAILY RELAXATION

How many times have you come to the end of a day where you didn't have a minute to yourself, only to realise you didn't achieve anything either? That's because you didn't use time effectively. To help you do so, there's one more list you need to make.

Not To Do list

You probably spent a considerable part of your day being side-tracked, time-wasting or engaged in some unproductive activity. That's why it makes sense to write a *Not To Do* list. This may sound silly, but again, this very act of writing things down helps you focus seriously on the areas you need to address. Perhaps you:

- flit from task to task without ever finishing one completely
- allow yourself to be interrupted by the telephone
- move things around unnecessarily
- don't have a clear idea of what you want to achieve daily
- watch too much television
- allow yourself to be side-tracked by trivia
- chat unnecessarily
- are indecisive.

If you recognise that you do some or all of the above things, reassure yourself that they are habits, and habits can be broken. You can address some of these issues immediately, and others with practice. You can make a pact with yourself to watch less television immediately, and by making lists you can have a clear idea of what you want to achieve every day. Next time you find yourself reaching for the post when you are already in the middle of something – stop. With practice you can soon get into the habit of completing one thing before starting another. Obviously your *Not To Do* list will reflect your lifestyle. If you work, your list will be different from someone who spends most of their day at home.

What if you work from home, however, and have important deadlines to meet – what could you write in your *Not To Do* list?

- I won't chat with friends on the telephone during the working day.
- I won't allow myself to be interrupted by personal callers.
- I won't make more than three drinks during the day.
- I won't be side-tracked by household chores or trivia.
- I won't consider domestic/personal issues during my working hours.

So, if friends telephone during your working hours, ask them to call later or offer to ring them when you've finished work. If they're true friends they'll respect your need to work and will soon stop interrupting you. And the same with other personal callers – be firm – if you respect your time, they will too.

You couldn't drink endless cups of tea if you were out in the workplace, or break off to put washing in the machine – so don't do it at home either. Unless you have made provision for that in your daily timetable. And if you have, keep to the time you've allowed to do it and don't end up doing a whole load of other chores as well.

INVESTING TIME

You have done something special. In spending time writing your own blueprint, plans and lists, you have invested time in yourself. You've considered what you want, how you're going to achieve it, and you've set aside time for yourself to do just that. And you've earmarked time to spend with your friends and family too; unhurried days which everyone will remember fondly. All this, because you took the time and trouble to plan and organise your days.

Becoming more organised

Now you are organised – keep it that way. Stick to the schedules and lists you've made. And don't forget to put aside a little free time every week to allow for the unexpected. This way when something really urgent crops us, you can slot it in without too much trouble.

Be self-disciplined. Once everyone sees how well you organise your life and time, they'll have a new-found respect for you, and rightly so.

Delegating

However well you organise your life, you are only human. Don't accept too much work because you can't say no. Ask others to help out at home and at work. You'll never know what anyone is capable of unless you give them a chance.

And when the going does get tough, use the 'Relaxing on the Go' exercise (page 25) to help keep you free of tension. And never do more than one thing at a time – start a task and stick with it – then cross it off your list.

Avoiding

How often have you avoided writing a letter or making a phone call because it was difficult? You put it off, and then the next day it was hanging over you again. Face these situations head on. Put them on your

To Do list and give them an A priority. And do it! Handle all unpleasant tasks this way. You'll feel so much better afterwards and will sail through the rest of your list with ease.

The other thing to avoid is interruptions. If you really don't want to be interrupted – don't answer the telephone or the door bell. You have a perfect right not to. If you are expecting an important call, screen incoming messages by having someone answer for you or use an answering machine. Alternatively you can always dial '1471' afterwards to see who called or invest in a gadget which displays the number of the person calling.

Admitting the truth

Beware of making excuses.

It's so easy to say, 'Well, the phone kept ringing and I just couldn't get a thing done'. Or, 'Billy phoned with a problem he wanted my advice about and it took longer than I thought'.

Are you sure you weren't just a little pleased that Billy called or the phone kept ringing? After all, whilst you're dealing with someone else's problems, you don't have to concentrate on your own tasks or challenges.

There are countless excuses you could give for not using your time effectively, but if you organise yourself, plan well, and stick to it, you won't need to make any.

Self-discipline

Making time for daily relaxation is essential. By following the steps outlined in this chapter, you will be able to set aside 20 minutes a day to relax, at the very least. More likely, you'll be able to schedule two relaxation sessions into your day – one in the morning and one at night. Some days, ideally, you'll manage three.

It will mean making changes – waking earlier, spending a little less time with friends or giving up half an hour's television a day. But if you truly want positive changes in your life, you have to make the effort. And that requires self-discipline.

CASE STUDY

Linda feels she's wasting time, but can't seem to fit more into her day

Linda, who's 25, works at the local car plant. Although she's happily married to John, a lab technician, she often feels she ought to be doing far more with her life. In her teens she used to paint watercolours of local scenes and this is something she'd like to do again, but she can never find the time. The evenings seem to whiz past. By the time they've eaten, washed up, tidied and watched a bit of television it's time for bed. And most weekends are taken up with shopping, DIY, visiting parents and the occasional night out.

After attending a course at work about time management, Linda decides to apply what she's learned to her life away from work – with amazing results. By scheduling her work, visits, shopping, DIY and everything else she does in a week, she is able to see where she was wasting time. Now, not only does she have the time to paint local scenes, she has a regular stall at a Sunday market where she sells them. Nothing else in her life has suffered as a result of her painting. In fact she seems to have more energy than ever. And, since attending a stress management course at work, Linda's also made time for regular relaxation.

KEY POINTS

- Forward planning is essential to organise your days and months effectively, and to make the most of your time.

- It is equally important to block in leisure time as well as work and more everyday chores.

- Make a conscious effort to avoid all those habits which eat into your day, such as watching too much TV; chatting idly on the telephone; moving bits of paper from one place to another.

- When you value your time, others will too.

ACTIVITY

Review your own habits by thinking of a day where you set out to do much, but achieved little. Think it through from start to finish, writing down all the things which prevented you from doing all you wanted. Now turn this into a *Things Not To Do* list.

5

Making Your Surroundings More Relaxing

Our surroundings affect us and our ability to relax. Furniture, air quality and lights all play their part in creating a harmonious environment. The colour of our walls influences our moods and feelings, as does noise, smell and the music we listen to.

ELIMINATING STRESS FACTORS

Few people have the luxury of living exactly where they wish in the house of their dreams. Financial restrictions, work commitments and family ties often make this difficult. But what you can do is to make your own surroundings as relaxing as possible. One of the first things you need to do is to eliminate, or reduce, stressful (or potentially stressful) factors.

Noise

By far the most pervasive environmental stress factor for everyone is noise. Whether the mind blocks it out or not, the body reacts to noise; everything from barking dogs and loud music to rows and traffic noise. And over long periods it can impair your ability to concentrate and cause you to become irritable and tense.

Reducing noise levels
Of course, it's not always possible to control the level of noise you're subjected to, but there are things you can do to lessen its impact.

With modern materials it is quite possible to reduce external noise considerably. Double glazing is one such option, and while secondary glazing may not be quite as effective it will cut noise levels and is much cheaper. Heavy curtains will make a difference too, and some have special linings which are designed specifically to reduce noise. There are also a variety of soundproofing materials on the market which can be applied to external or internal walls.

The other option is to consider ways of covering the noise with a more relaxing sound such as soft tranquil music.

Reducing noise in the garden

To see and hear running water is therapeutic. A water feature in your garden also gives the added bonus of helping to block out unwelcome noise such as traffic when you're trying to have a quiet relaxing break in the open air. Bubble pools, fountains and running water features can be bought from garden centres or made in any size, making them suitable for even the tiniest yard or garden.

Hedging is a more effective barrier to noise than fencing, and if you live near a busy road you'll also find it absorbs pollution and vibration better too. It provides a far more pleasing and natural backdrop to your garden than fencing and, depending on which variety you choose, will have the added bonus of offering visual interest all year round.

Lighting

Being in constant artificial light is not good for any of us. Natural light regulates melanonin levels which in turn affect our mood, sleep and, in women, their reproductive cycle. If you don't get enough natural daylight, your melanonin levels build up and you'll experience loss of energy and possibly experience depressive moods. During the winter, when periods of natural daylight are reduced and longer is spent in artificial light, people can find themselves affected by Seasonal Affective Disorder (SAD).

If you do need to live and work in an artificially-lit environment, consider changing to chromalux lighting.

Help yourself:

● avoid fluorescent lighting

● work close to natural light (near windows)

● go outside as often as possible.

Air

Air quality is essential to good health. Within the atmosphere all around us are electrically-charged molecules known as ions. As we breathe we inhale these ions, although some are absorbed through the skin.

If the air becomes charged with too many positive ions our physical and psychological well-being can be adversely affected. We may experience lethargy, irritability, depression, headaches and breathing problems. Alternatively, in an area with a relatively high negative ion count, such as at a seaside, we will feel much better.

De-ionising

The severity to which people react to ion imbalances varies from person to person, but it makes sense for everyone to be aware of what leads to a build up of positive ions in the atmosphere. Pollutants (including cigarette smoke and car fumes), central heating, air conditioning and overcrowding will result in a build up of positive ions. This is also the case just before a thunderstorm.

Whenever possible try to keep your home well-ventilated and open windows. You might consider purchasing an ioniser as this will output healthy negative ions to keep the air in your home fresh and clear.

Humidifying

In many homes the air is too dry and this can lead to dry sore throats, sinus trouble and breathing problems. To help maintain good levels of humidity place bowls of water in your rooms along with plants and vases of flowers. You can buy a gauge which measures humidity levels in your home, and if necessary an electric humidifying unit to prevent the air becoming too dry.

Clutter

If your home is always full of clutter and mess, make a pact with yourself to get it tidied. Much psychological stress is caused by having a home which is untidy, cluttered and disorganised. It leads to irritability, lethargy and anger, and much wasted time searching for things you've 'lost'.

'A place for everything and everything in its place', may be an old-fashioned saying, but it doesn't make it any less true. To be efficient and to have an environment which is conducive to relaxation, you need to be organised.

Organising

Whether you are at home all day or at work all day you need to organise your home. Ideally, tidy your home as you go – wash up as you cook and after meals, clean washbasins after use, and iron and hang up clothes before you need them. Buy a communal wash basket so items of clothing don't get left on floors and buy or make specific storage areas for everyday items such as newspapers, and files for all your paperwork including bills and receipts. Have rotas for jobs if other people live with you and carry out all housework routinely. You'll feel better once your home is uncluttered and it'll be a far better place in which to relax.

Avoiding extremes

Yes, it's great to have a tidy home, but it really doesn't matter if the bed's unmade once in a while, or if you dash off to the pictures without washing the dishes. Don't become obsessive about tidiness or cleanliness.

CHOOSING RELAXING COLOURS

Traditional associations of colour

Red   danger, blood, fire, sunset, warmth, love, passion, medicine, activity

Yellow   cowardice, jealousy, sun, radiance, gaiety, joy, sharpness

Green   fields, youth, fertility, growth, bad luck, tranquillity, envy

Blue   contemplation, coolness, recession, heaven, sadness, sky, sea

The above shows how, traditionally, we've associated certain colours with specific emotions and objects In heraldry too, colours were symbolic. Yellow and gold symbolised honour and loyalty; red symbolised courage and zeal, and purple was a symbol of royalty or high rank.

Mood enhancing colours

Whatever we have been formally taught about colour, we all have our own preferences, the colours we feel drawn to when choosing clothes or decorating a room. Research shows that different colours can impact our behaviour, moods and therefore our ability to relax. The impact may be subtle in some cases, profound in others. Being in blue light can lead to a lowering of blood pressure, for example, whilst being in red light can cause blood pressure to increase. So, whilst colour may be only one part of creating a relaxing environment, it is nonetheless a very important one.

Blue interior

Ranging from a powdery blue through to violet and purple, blue is a relaxing choice to use in a home. Blue aids sleep and reduces tension and violet represents inner balance and peace. The natural light of a room affects the colour, so if the blue you've chosen looks cold, try another until you get it right. Blue pigments build up in a room, so they'll look more intense if used on every wall. Greyish blues are easy to live with. Blues with a pink tinge such as purple may work better in small amounts.

Blue works well with most colours. Blue and yellow is cheerful, blue and green looks as nature intended, and shades of red, pink and orange will add warmth. A classic look is achieved when blue is complemented with white or cream

Yellow interior
Yellow rooms look warm and welcoming, so yellow is good for rooms which face north or don't have much natural light. Soft primrose yellows give a spring-like feel. Be careful which you choose as a yellow with a greeny tinge will clash with warm orange-based yellows and can be irritating. More than any other colour, yellow changes under electric light. For this reason take home fabric swatches or samples to test on your walls.

Grey, white or blue works wonderfully against yellow. But be careful about the depth of contrasting colour. A strong blue may overwhelm a pastel yellow, but work wonderfully with a deep strong yellow. Red against yellow can give a rich opulent effect, whilst pink can look modern. As a general rule, reds and pinks work best with warm yellows.

Red interior
Red can stimulate and warm. It can also make walls appear closer, making a room feel oppressive. Decorators sometimes use it in rooms which are passed through such as halls or foyers, but in main rooms it is used chiefly to highlight.

Green is the classic foil to red, although gold picture frames look exquisite. To cool down a red room, a few spots of blue will help, whereas white makes red instantly more casual. Like red, orange can also reduce space and appear stifling unless used carefully.

Green interior
Although green goes with almost anything, it can make you feel sluggish. You will usually need to use warm highlights such as red or yellow to prevent a cold institutional look. This is especially true if green is used in a north-facing room.

Pink interior
Pink is normally associated with composure and tranquillity. Its shades range from brownish pinks to candy pastels. When used with white, pink creates an innocent look and feel. Pink works well with neutrals, beige, brown and grey.

White interiors
White is traditionally associated with purity and peace. Because light and space are so important many people choose to paint walls white or off-white. The effect of this varies from person to person – some find it calming, others find it irritating. White can look fresh but it may also appear bland, cold and clinical.

Neutral interiors
Beigey-browns are considered to be intimate. Greys can be gentle providing they're a blue-grey rather than an ash-grey. Neutrals are flexible but do need the addition of colour to give them a lift. Most colours go with neutrals but it is best to stick with one or two accents rather than a hotchpotch of diverse colours which may cause a confusing effect.

Colour tips
Colours divide into warm tones and cool tones:

● reds, oranges, pinks and golden yellows are warm (these tones create warm, bright effects but can make rooms appear smaller)

● blue, green and very citrus yellows are cool (these have a spaciousness about them but can appear cold). The effects of various colours differ from person to person. Follow your instincts and have fun experimenting.

SELECTING FURNITURE FOR RELAXATION

You buy furniture according to your budget and personal taste. But badly designed furniture can cause you to adopt poor posture which will lead to tension in areas of your body and poor breathing. It's amazing how quickly your body will adapt to badly designed chairs, desks, worktops, beds and sofas. Your shoulders may hunch and you could begin stooping. This won't happen overnight, but will occur gradually as your body adapts to the posture you frequently adopt.

The golden rule is to test furniture before you buy.

Beds

Don't feel embarrassed about lying on a bed in a shop. You will spend years in the bed you choose – literally – so you need to make sure it supports you correctly. There are some wonderful beds and mattresses on the market, some even take into account the weight difference between you and your partner and compensate accordingly. Ensure the mattress gives your back firm support and follows your body's contours. Buy the best bed and mattress your budget will stretch to and look upon it as investment in your future health.

Chairs

There are many new types of chair which encourage good posture habits. When choosing a chair, consider the following:

● It's important your feet reach the ground. If they don't, use a foot rest.

● Make sure the seat is deep enough to reach just before your knees as this offers proper support to your thighs.

● Choose well-padded chairs to avoid placing pressure on soft tissues.

With all furniture and fittings around your home, testing is the key. Buy things that are attractive and pleasing to you personally but consider the practicalities too. If you're taller or shorter than average, you may consider altering your worktop heights for example, or putting up shelving that is wider rather than taller to avoid excessive stretching or bending.

CREATING PERSONAL SPACE AT WORK

Unless you work from home, you will probably spend much of your life in an environment that someone else has created. An office or warehouse maybe, or on the road every day, travelling between customers or delivering and collecting goods.

Your workplace has to be efficient and, according to your job and position, there may not be too much space that you can truly call your own. It may be that you have your own office, however, or work at a particular desk every day. Perhaps you drive the same van to and from customers. If that's the case, there are things you can do to personalise that space and make it more enjoyable to be in.

Improving general workspace

The place where you work will contribute to your overall well-being and affect your mood. You may love your job, but if it takes place in ugly uninspiring surroundings the quality of your work will suffer. And this will impact on your life away from work. It makes sense therefore to do all you can to make your working days as enjoyable as possible.

Consider brightening your general work space by:

- bringing in fresh flowers to brighten your office or a nearby windowsill
- using favourite pot plants to cheer surroundings
- hanging paintings or posters
- opening windows whenever practical
- getting rid of excess clutter
- operating a no-smoking policy
- keeping air fresh with an air ioniser.

Whatever you do, however, ensure you work in accordance with health and safety procedures. A vase of flowers next to electrical equipment or trailing flexes could prove disastrous, so check guidelines.

Immediate surroundings

Your desk, lorry cab, briefcase or workbench can be home to more personal items. Perhaps you have a desire to visit New York – how about putting up a travel poster of the Big Apple next to your desk? Or if New Orleans is more your sort of place, gather jazz tapes to play in your cab.

Whatever your work situation – you can do much to personalise it, even if only in very small ways:

- use pens, mugs and desk tidies of your choice
- put small pictures in frames – snapshots of loved ones and places you enjoy visiting
- find a picture which always makes you laugh or smile and keep it handy
- use amusing post-it notes to send messages to colleagues or reminders to yourself
- place motivational statements where you can see them – such as *Only 10 More Sales Needed To Reach Record Target – Yes!*
- pin up postcards.

Remember to take down dog-eared pictures and cards and not to clutter your workspace or all your good intentions will be lost.

ENJOYING PERSONAL SPACE AT HOME

At home your surroundings can reflect the true you. Maybe not all of your home, because if you live with others it's only fair that some compromises are made. But whether you have a whole house to yourself or part of a bedroom, you need an area which you can call your own. Some personal space. Use your imagination and don't be swayed by others – surround yourself with furniture, fabrics, colours, items which please you.

Screening

Physical screening
Look at the amount of room you have available for personal space. A place where you can relax, meditate, exercise, read, study or listen to music. If you can't have a complete room – consider screening an area of the room. A screen needn't be a solid floor to ceiling partition but may be a folding screen which you can put away when not in use or when you need to use the entire room. Make or find a screen which appeals to you. Consider natural materials such as wood or bamboo or cover in a pleasing fabric. A bare wood screen covered in photographs, concert tickets, or other memorabilia is a great way to evoke fond memories, or you could cover it with inspirational sayings and affirmation. Books on decoupage will show you the best way to go about this.

Alternatively you could place a rug in a corner of the room and place one or two decorative potted ferns around the area to define this as your space.

Carrying a 'screen'
It's worth remembering however that practising relaxation on a regular basis allows you to carry personal space with you at all times. Even in the midst of crowds or chaos you'll be able to concentrate and exude a certain calmness. This is a truly wonderful state to attain.

Another way of doing this is to imagine yourself surrounded by a glass screen, like being in a protective dome. Next time you're in a room where there are people chatting and a TV blaring, or on crowded public transport perhaps, try the following:

● take a few deep breaths

● visualise a glass barrier forming all around you

● drop your shoulders

● breathe slower and deeper

● smile.

Be careful not to fool yourself into thinking you operate better in a chaotic environment than you do. The above exercise is really helpful and used by many, but remember, we all need peace, quiet and personal space sometimes.

Working at home

Working from home poses fresh challenges even if you are fortunate enough to have a dedicated room to operate from. To avoid the area (and your mind) becoming cluttered, organisation is the key. If you often need to refer to certain information, pin it up where you can see it without having to rummage through lots of other paper. Put motivational statements where you can see them too, for those moments when you'd rather be anywhere else but there!

If space permits, a small filing cabinet is useful, or a box file. Keep your desk 'worklike' too. Don't let home effects stray onto it. And keep the floor free of clutter 'you need to be able to move around freely and easily.

Your office
In general your 'office' needs to be:

● well-ventilated

● a room you're comfortable in

● a comfortable temperature – not too hot

● pleasantly decorated so it provides additional interest in think breaks

● clutter free.

Choose restful colours and fabrics for your office decor and anti-static floor covering if possible. Have things around you which you like and, if practical, have access to music – although not from another room.

Chair
Choose your chair carefully. Ideally it should have:

● a five-castor base to give maximum stability and manoeuvrability

● height adjustable seat and back

● an adjustable back float

● well padded seat and back

- a deep seat which reaches to just before your knees

- no arms, or height adjustable arms which must be able to fit under the desk surface.

If your feet don't touch the floor when you've adjusted the chair, use a foot rest. Sit close into your desk (to avoid unnecessary stretching), allowing your weight to be evenly spread across the body and shoulders, with your hips parallel to your desk or keyboard to avoid keeping your body at an unnatural angle.

Desk

- Working surface needs to be waist height.

- It must be deep enough to support a computer at correct distance – which is about arm's length,

- There should be plenty of leg room giving unrestricted movement.

- The desk should have a matt non-reflective surface – not highly glossed or polished.

Out of sight, out of mind
Wherever possible, keep your working environment separate from your home environment. It's difficult to relax in the evenings if you're still facing the pile of paperwork you should have finished yesterday. Create a situation where you can 'close the door' on your work – even if it's simply sliding a screen in front of your desk or throwing a blanket over box files. Operate an out of sight, out of mind policy once you're finished for the day.

CASE STUDY

Harry knew he was working inefficiently, and was paying the price

When Harry first joined the consultancy, it was only in its infancy and cash was short. The office was a large room attached to the head consultant's house and the surroundings were not ideal. Harry's 'desk' was an old oak table, the shelves were bookcases moved in from another part of the house, and the fax, computer and printer stood on top of an old pasting table. The chairs were old dining chairs, too. The head consultant assured Harry that when cash flow improved he would purchase dedicated office furniture.

As the weeks progressed, the workload grew and Harry found it increasingly difficult to manage with such resources. Everything seemed to take twice as long because it was so makeshift. His back and shoulders started getting painful too – something he'd never experienced before.

Finally, in desperation, Harry gave his boss an ultimatum – either the furniture was replaced by dedicated office furniture or he'd be forced to leave. Begrudgingly a supplier was contacted and office furniture bought in – a desk, swivel chair, computer desk, fax and printer stand and shelving systems. It wasn't long, however, before Harry's boss was congratulating himself. Not only were they working quicker and more efficiently, the pains in Harry's back and shoulders had gone!

KEY POINTS

- Work on reducing noise levels, improving air quality and maintaining good levels of humidity.

- Keep your environment well-ventilated and eliminate clutter.

- Use colour thoughtfully – it can have an impact on your behaviour, moods and ability to relax.

- Choose furniture for your long-term comfort as well as its practicality.

- Try to personalise some space for yourself at work.

- If you work from home try to keep your work out of sight when you have finished for the day.

ACTIVITY

Which part of your house or flat do you relax in? How could you make it more relaxing? Consider lighting, colour, furniture, screening, fabrics and noise. Write your ideas down, noting any particular challenges. For each challenge, come up with five ways you could work around them.

Completed? Congratulations! Why not put the ideas on your *To Do* list (page 48)?

6

Relaxing Your Way to Sleep

Sleep is a completely natural function and one which we will spend up to one-third of our lives doing. People need differing amounts of sleep, however, so don't become over-concerned because you don't get a full eight hours every night or because your neighbour appears to get by on only two! You'll probably find your own sleep needs vary too. Some weeks, six hours a night may have you waking refreshed, while at other times you need more.

LINKING RELAXATION AND SLEEP

Sleep is essential if you are to work well and enjoy life as it allows your mind and body to rest and recuperate. Disturbed sleep is often a sign of stress and a continued lack of sleep will lead to a wide range of health problems. Not getting enough sleep can often result in further anxiety as you worry about your lack of sleep – and so the cycle continues.

Disturbed sleep can take different forms, including:

- having difficulty getting to sleep

- waking after an hour or so and being unable to get back to sleep

- waking after six or so hours still feeling extremely tired

- sleeping fitfully.

Transient insomnia occurs when you have a disturbance in your routine. People who work on shifts or travel through different time zones may experience this. If you have a row with someone or have troubles at work or suffer some other emotional upset you may then suffer short-term insomnia. Long-term insomnia occurs when you have more severe, deep-rooted problems and you need to take steps to overcome or resolve these problems.

Conforming to demands

How often do you go to sleep when you choose and wake up at the time you want to? Rarely, probably never. Today, more than ever, pressure is placed upon you to conform. To get up and travel to work or college, do shopping, or whatever your day involves whether that's housework, taking children to school or some other commitment. This means that you are waking at the times demanded by those activities, not by the needs of your body.

Relaxing during the day

Your working life can be difficult. Not only do you have to perform well to keep your job, you may also have financial worries, or problems with personal relationships. By the end of a day where no provision is made for you to relax either you're likely to be overtired and agitated. It's not surprising therefore that stress results in 85% of industrial accidents, and 60% of crashes involve company cars.

Most societies do not make provision for periods of relaxation during the working day. Jack Black in his book, *Mindstore,* says: 'If only we could see the sense in building relaxation breaks into the culture of every profession and business in this country we would save a fortune on health expenditure, freeing vital resources for where they are needed most. If only it were taught in every school to make it a way of life … The effects of stress may be the number one issue today. The solution – relaxation – must become our primary concern.'

Fortunately, progressive companies realise the benefits of introducing relaxation breaks into their company culture and this is likely to become a growing trend. Relaxing during the day is good for you. Companies pay their workforce to take relaxation breaks because it gives them an improved workforce.

If you have trouble sleeping, you can often compensate for disturbed sleep by engaging in relaxation or meditation during the day. Or have a nap. This will not make your night-time sleep more disturbed as is sometimes suggested. On the contrary, by restoring a degree of relaxation to your body, it will improve your night-time sleep.

Releasing habits

Are you one of those people who wouldn't dream of taking a nap in the daytime? If not, why not? Were you raised with the idea that it's lazy to nap during the day so you stay awake regardless of how much or how little you have to do? The result is that when you come to sleep at night you'll find it difficult, despite being extremely tired. Imagine the confusion your body clock is in.

Napping in the day has been shown to have other benefits too. Studies in Greece found that people at risk from coronary heart disease reduced their risk of heart attack by as much as 30% simply by taking a half-hour nap in the afternoon.

So, if you can't nap during the day or in your lunch hour, review the chapter on relaxation exercises (Chapter 2) and make time to practise relaxation during the day. Just 20 minutes deep relaxation is equivalent to two hours sleep!

AVOIDING STIMULATING FOODS

Eating certain foods can contribute to insomnia, especially if eaten during the evening or last thing at night. Because of this, sleeplessness can often be normalised simply by looking at your diet and eliminating certain foods and drinks.

Drinks
Reduce caffeine rich drinks such as tea, coffee, cola and chocolate. There are many tea alternatives such as RedBush tea which is naturally caffeine free, low in tannin, and available in tea-bag form. Alternatively, try one of a wide variety of herbal teas such as camomile, hop or lemon verbena teas which make a good bedtime drink and have relaxing properties. Then, of course, there's always water. Contrary to popular belief, alcohol doesn't aid sleep either, so you need to reduce your intake of alcohol if insomnia is a problem.

Vitamins
Many insomniacs have been found to have low vitamin B levels (B1, B2, B3, B6, B12) which can indicate a poor diet. The B vitamins help your body cope with stress which is a major cause of insomnia. They help your nervous system function correctly which in turn impacts on your overall wellness. Wholegrain cereals, bananas, avocados, nuts, seeds and wholemeal bread are rich in vitamin B. Western diets rarely contain enough vitamin B, but you can obtain B Complex tablets from your chemist or local health store.

Foods
Avoid a diet of sugary or starchy foods. Refined sugar can cause fluctuations in your blood sugar levels and waking during the night is often due to a sudden drop in blood sugar level. Replace refined sugar by complex carbohydrates such as wholemeal bread, wholewheat pasta and cereals. Eat plenty of fresh fruit and vegetables as research has found that many insomniacs lack these in their diet; cook them for as little time as possible.

Try and eat your last meal around three hours before you go to bed to give your system time to digest the food. This will help you sleep better. Eating an evening meal high in complex carbohydrates will also help you to avoid waking during the night through hunger.

Tryptophan
Tryptophan, found in many foods, has been shown to play a significant part in normal sleep. It is an amino acid which produces a substance in the body called serotonin which can initiate sleep. Try eating foods in which tryptophan is present, such as:

● cottage and other cheese

● yogurt

● chicken

● fish

● seafood

● baked beans

● nuts (almonds, brazils, peanuts, pecans, walnuts)

● milk

● bananas

● rice

● pasta

● eggs

● meat

● wheatgerm

● brewer's yeast

● seeds (pumpkin, sunflower, sesame)

● lima and other dried beans

● chickpeas.

In every gram of milk there is around 15mg of tryptophan. So, drinking a tumbler of warm milk before bedtime provides roughly a 'prescription' dose; as does an ounce or two of sesame, sunflower or pumpkin seeds; and nuts, or an egg or a bowl of yogurt.

DEVELOPING SLEEP PATTERNS

We often establish patterns or rituals associated with sleep. If you've been doing things a certain way for a long period of time you may not even recognise them as patterns, but if they vary your sleep can often become disturbed. These could include things like:

- bathing

- putting clothes away

- reading

- listening to music

- listening to the radio

- praying

- sex

- position in which you sleep.

Altering your pre-bed routine

If you're having trouble sleeping, look at what things were part of your pre-sleep ritual and how they've changed. Perhaps you used to bathe last thing at night, but have switched to rising early and having a shower instead. Have you recently started sleeping alone, watching television until the early hours, eating toast and tea in bed, listening to late night news, sleeping with a lamp on, shutting your bedroom window, reading in bed or walking the dog last thing at night?

It may not be possible (or desirable) to reintroduce some of your old habits into your bedtime routine, so the key is not to worry. Follow the guidelines in this chapter and eventually they will become your new ritual.

Bedroom only
It's worth remembering that everyone has their own preferences and what suits you may not suit another. Some sleeping guides recommend you use your bedroom for sleeping only – no reading and certainly no watching television. The theory is that you will associate your bedroom with sleep alone. But this wouldn't suit the large numbers of people who enjoy reading in bed, for example, and who sleep perfectly well.

Avoid mental stimulation
Try not to let your mind become too stimulated before going to bed.

● If you find the evening news depressing – give it up. Catch up with the world's events the following morning.

● If you have negative thoughts whirring around in your head, write them down and tell yourself you'll deal with them at 10 o'clock tomorrow morning (or whenever you have ten minutes spare). This way you're not ignoring things, you're simply choosing to deal with them at a more appropriate time.

● Think of positive affirmations as you lie in bed, such as: *I am drifting into a deep sound sleep* or *I am warm, comfortable and sleepy.*

Physical exercise
If you've suddenly taken to running last thing at night and now find you can't sleep, change to running in the morning or afternoon. Exercise is good for you and helps promote sleep, so do develop an exercise routine.

Visualisation
The power of visualisation was outlined in Chapter 3 and is often a valuable aid to sleep. When Jane's dog died she was understandably distraught and had trouble sleeping. She missed the late night dog walks too. Not wanting to go out alone late at night she began to visualise the walks.

'It worked wonders,' Jane said. 'I lay in bed and, after relaxing, would visualise taking Sam for his late-night walk. I imagined myself walking along the lane and experienced the journey in great detail. I would smell the damp earth and shrubs, hear the chink of his lead as he walked, and visualise the late night sky.'

Far from finding this a distressing experience, Jane found it helped tremendously and she would often drop off to sleep long before she got back from her 'dog walk'. Now her sleep pattern is restored she no longer finds visualisation necessary, but remains convinced it helped her through a difficult period.

Programming your mind
Programme your mind to help you instead of having it work against you. Talk about sleep in a positive way. Avoid saying, 'I can never get to sleep at night', or 'I always get up two our three times during the night'. Set aside time to visualise yourself sleeping well every night and practise it regularly – not just once our twice. It's taken you a long time to get into certain habits, so allow yourself time to move away from them.

WAKING REFRESHED

Many people wake up feeling as though they haven't slept even though they have. This is known as pseudo insomnia and can be caused by medication.

Medication

Some people, in desperation, turn to their doctor for sleeping tablets In some cases where the underlying causes warrant it, this may be necessary. Some of these tablets can be addictive, however, and have side-effects ranging from indigestion and rashes to raised blood pressure and breathing problems. All sleeping tablets deal only with the symptom of sleeplessness – they do not deal with the cause of insomnia. For this reason doctors are often reluctant to prescribe them. Besides, they do not help you sleep – they knock you out, which is something quite different and explains why you wake feeling unrefreshed. And the trouble with sleeping tablets is that once you stop taking them they can lead to worse insomnia.

Natural products
There are many natural products available in health stores to help you through a bout of disturbed sleep. They are non-habit forming and so can be easily left off once you've dealt with the cause of your insomnia. Dolomite, calcium and passiflora are linked with sleep and can often be found in capsule form. There is also a range of safe, natural pills which can be taken in lesser doses in the day to aid relaxation and again at night to induce sleep. Many essential oils have calming, sedative qualities too, including: camomile, sandalwood, valerian, lavender and yarrow. Try putting a couple of drops of lavender onto your pillow at night or putting ten drops into a hot bath before you retire to make you feel pleasantly drowsy.

Plan for the following day

The moment you wake, even before you open your eyes, the day and what it holds dawns with you. Much of how you feel will depend on what you're doing that day and how well you've planned it. Whether you're going to work or college, staying at home, going shopping or visiting relatives, take a few minutes the evening before to prepare. This avoids the mental fog of first thoughts, such as 'What shall I wear?'

Use the early part of the evening to think about what you need tomorrow. What you're going to wear. Is it washed and ironed? One of the reasons for waking unrefreshed is lack of planning. You'll wake up feeling more refreshed knowing that your clothes are ready, you've got plenty of time for breakfast, and that everything you need for the day is ready for you to pick up when you walk out the door.

Use up your energy
To use up your energy, make love or get up and leave your bedroom and do something around the house. Some people believe their subconscious doesn't want them to sleep when they can't. So, if you enjoy writing – go and write. If you paint – go and paint. Or write a long overdue letter to someone, or complete a task around the house. What you will find is that when you go back to bed you will fall asleep quicker and wake at the normal time, happy that you achieved something in the night instead of lying there worrying about not sleeping.

Checklist: What you can do in that short term

● Wear ear plugs if noise is a problem.

● Reduce your intake of alcohol and caffeine.

● Open a bedroom window.

● Avoid mental stimulation last thing at night.

● Increase tryptophan intake via foods.

● Use calming essential oils.

● Plan for the following day.

● Relax regularly.

● Practise visualisation at bedtime.

● Use up your energy.

Checklist: What you can do in the longer term

● Practise relaxation at least twice daily (three times ideally) for at least 15 minutes each time.

● Take more daily exercise.

● Buy a better bed or mattress.

● Enjoy regular aromatherapy sessions or massage to relax your muscles.

● Enjoy a better, more nutritional diet.

● Take a good long hard look at your lifestyle – are you living how you *really* want to?

What was your answer to the last point? Are you living how you want and doing the things you *truly* want? Be completely honest with yourself about this, as disturbed sleep is one of the most striking symptoms of stress. If the answer is no, then take a step towards changing it – today!

CASE STUDY

Sam's nights were disturbed

It had been a long time since Sam had enjoyed a good night's sleep. When he was first with his partner, Helen, he'd slept well. But as their relationship drifted into a rut he found himself spending much of the night awake. Now, with her gone completely, there were nights he didn't sleep at all, and his work was suffering.

Initially, his doctor refused to give him sleeping tablets, but when the problem continued, he was offered a short course. It didn't really help because although he slept, he woke feeling awful. Reading an article about insomnia in a magazine he tried some of the tips they suggested – took more exercise, reduced the amount of alcohol and tea and coffee he drank – and it did improve things, slightly.

One evening, after a particularly arduous day at work, he realised his life couldn't continue as it was. He was in a job which gave him no satisfaction; his life seemed to lack direction and, if he was honest, he missed Helen like mad. Forcing himself to ring her was one of the most difficult things Sam had ever done. But it was worth it as they're back together. Sam's also applying for different jobs and now has no trouble sleeping.

KEY POINTS

● Everyone needs differing amounts of sleep, and your needs will vary too.

● Practising relaxation daily aids sleep.

● Avoid stimulating food and drink.

● Reduce your alcohol intake.

● Check that your preparation for bed is helping you to relax and not the opposite.

ACTIVITY

Many people wake at their chosen time each day never having set an alarm clock or requested an early morning call. There are many ways of programming yourself to do this and the following is just one. Preferably do this before your relaxation exercise.

1. Make yourself comfortable in bed, then close your eyes.

2. Take several deep breaths.

3. Imagine a large clock covering the whole of the wall opposite your bed (it may be a digital clock or a traditional type with hands).

4. Notice the hands or digits moving around and coming to a stop at the time you wish to awaken.

5. When the hands rest on your chosen time, affirm to yourself, 'This is the time I will waken, refreshed'.

Don't rush the exercise; take five or more minutes to complete it. And don't set an alarm clock just in case! Many people use this method (or a variation) to great effect, and never set an alarm again.

7

Travelling Relaxed

Not so long ago it would have taken over a week to travel to the north of the country from the south. The journey would certainly have been uncomfortable and fraught with danger. Bogs and highwaymen would have been a constant threat amid the added worries of horses losing shoes and carriages their wheels.

Now we can drive in a warm car to our local airport in the morning and catch a plane which will have us at our destination by midday. And the comfort in which we travel has never been better. In warm surroundings we can snack and drink without having to move from our comfy upholstered seats. Yet still people complain about having to check in an hour before to just sit and wait.

VIEWING TRAVEL DIFFERENTLY

As travel methods become more efficient, journey times lessen. We can travel by car, aeroplane, hovercraft, ship, train, bus, helicopter, coach or ferry. But instead of using the time saved to sit back and do nothing, many of us cram in another meeting or take on yet more commitments.

If you're going on holiday – view the travel as part of the holiday. From the time you pack the suitcases in the car or catch a taxi to the train station – adopt a holiday mood. Leave earlier if possible and stop off for regular breaks and snacks. Refuse to let anything get you down – after all, you're on your hols!

Losing control

Travel is often viewed as a means to an end, a way from A to B. And if you're travelling to a meeting or work that's often all it can be – or is it? There's no denying many forms of travel can be stressful, especially during the rush hour in driving rain or dense fog. And there is so much out of your control, especially if you're not in the driving seat. You can meet roadworks, face delays at airports, diversions which take you miles out of your way, ferry cancellations or late sailings, or you could break down.

Lack of control over your journey can result in you losing control. You've surely seen people in traffic jams drumming their fingers impatiently on the steering wheel. Or frantically doing U-turns to find an alternative route. You've heard people at airports, stations and ferry terminals almost crying with frustration at yet another delay. Perhaps you're one of those people – in which case you need to start viewing travel differently – whatever mode of transport you're using.

Triggering a damaging response

Perfectly mild mannered people can turn into aggressive road hogs once behind the wheel of their car. They vent their pent-up frustration on other road users (who, after all, don't know them) as a way of letting off steam whilst feeling relatively safe cocooned in their metal boxes. The trouble is they occasionally meet their match, sometimes with tragic results.

Bodily response

Your body can't distinguish from a physical threat or a mental one (as outlined in Chapter 1). So, every time you tense up and sense outrage at yet another hiccup in your journey plans, you can trigger the fight or flight response. Because you cannot flee from your 'attacker' (the traffic jam) you may switch to the fight response and begin thumping the steering wheel and becoming aggressive.

Or are you someone who hides their feelings and doesn't show outward signs of stress? Next time you're travelling, check to see if:

● your teeth are clenched

● your hands are clenched (are you gripping the steering wheel unnecessarily tightly?)

● your shoulders are tense.

If the answer is yes, begin to relax those areas and see how differently you feel. Whatever you're doing, get used to scanning your body for tension, and when you find it – relax those areas.

De-stressing travel

As travel is inevitable, why not make a pact with yourself to view it differently? During a stress management workshop one attendee said that travel was the one area which wound her up the most. She felt she couldn't handle it when confronted with a traffic queue when she was already, and invariably, late. Another lady from a different culture smiled and said they were so used to vehicles breaking down, they simply accepted it as a way of life. Who do you think has the healthiest response?

So, it's not what happens to you when you're travelling, it's how you react to it that matters. And that often means taking a deep breath and accepting the things you cannot change.

Relaxing on the go
Wherever and however you're travelling, practise relaxation and visualisation techniques before and after the journey, although you can, of course, practise some relaxation techniques as you travel. The following exercise, mentioned in Chapter 2, can be done even if you're driving.

1. Shrug your shoulders several times before dropping them.

2. Be aware of your pulse and your breathing.

3. Relax your jaw, letting your lips part slightly.

4. Breathe in through your nose.

5. Breathe out (loudly and explosively if possible, if not just say 'let go' to yourself as you do it).

6. Do this a few more times, then breathe more slowly and deeply.

7. Smile.

What's great about this technique is that it can be done anywhere – on a plane, in a car, even on a bus crowded with people – and is a quick and easy way to relieve sudden 'nerves' and tension.

Travel alternatives
Public transport
If you always use your car – why not try public transport if it's an option? It's amazing how many people enjoy travelling on buses and trains after stubbornly using their cars for years. You can sit back whilst someone else does all the driving, and, although it may not be as convenient, you'll rediscover many other things. People, for one. Strike up conversations and interact with people. Many friendships have been formed this way and you'll be amazed at the diversity of people you'll meet. Besides, its environmentally more acceptable.

Sharing cars
If you travel to and from work regularly, find out how many other people come from your area. Ask them if they'd be interested in sharing a car on a regular basis. This is also an environmentally friendly option which

makes good sense for your finances too. But again, the social interaction is important. You'd be amazed at the tremendous sense of camaraderie that can be spawned from such simple ideas.

Travelling free
There is, of course, a cost-free way of travelling that you'd be sensible to rediscover – walking and cycling. Getting yourself physically fit is a first step towards helping your body avoid stress rather than adapt to it. It does mean you have to think ahead more, but the benefits will far outweigh that. You'll be surprised at just how much more you'll notice on your journey, and you can wind down lanes, alleys and passages and discover a world you didn't even know existed right on your own doorstep. And again, it's far more sociable. You'll meet people on their way to work, walking dogs, collecting children from school, or out on their daily shopping trip. So give walking and cycling a go. It is the ultimate way to help your environment and has the enormous benefit of helping you get fit.

OVERCOMING OBSTACLES AND FEARS

Almost everyone fears something and it is quite reasonable and healthy for us to fear some situations. If you were confronted by an attacker for instance, fear and anxiety would be a perfectly natural response and would aid your survival.

But there are many situations people fear which cannot be considered reasonable. Some people fear the thought of driving a car, the colour green, crossing water, travelling by train or entering tall buildings. The situations are not essentially dangerous but they can leave people feeling afraid and anxious – sometimes even unable to function. Often fears are totally irrational and have a stressful effect not only on the person themselves but on their colleagues, friends and families

Acknowledging fear

Many people have irrational fears about travelling, whether on public transport, ferries, motorways or aeroplanes. George used to tell everyone he was quite content to holiday in Britain every year. He believed it himself for a long time until a friend, who was not long back from America, told George about a trip he'd taken across the Grand Canyon.

'I realised then,' George said, 'that I'd been kidding myself I wanted to travel as much as the next person, but I had a terrible fear of flying.'

The good news is that many people have overcome such obstacles, spurred on by the realisation that they were missing out on so much in life.

Interfering with performance
Many jobs today involve travel. But if you have a fear of flying, or travelling on motorways, for example, this limits your choice of job and your chances of promotion. And, if you're self-employed it severely restricts your business activities and overall efficiency.

By identifying your fear and learning to manage the anxiety it causes, you can stop the fear undermining you in your personal and working life.

Learning fear
Many fears are learned, which is how you may come to fear something which is harmless and neither threatening or non-threatening. It's worth remembering that fear is not always helpful or necessary for your survival and is not always rational either. Fear will interfere with your life and can undermine your confidence, making it difficult for you to achieve your true potential.

Unlearning fear
But just as you are conditioned to produce fear and anxiety you can be pre-conditioned to overcome these things. You can unlearn how you have responded in the past. The following exercise has proved successful in helping people overcome fear and anxiety. But just as everyone learns at their own pace, it's worth remembering we *relearn* at our own pace too. If you are experiencing general anxiety or pronounced personal problems, however, talk with your doctor first as the following exercise may not be suitable for you.

Exercise to help overcome fear
You can do the following exercise with any thing or situation which frightens you, but for the purposes of this chapter, let's imagine you have a fear of flying. Get yourself a pad and pen and set aside some time in a quiet place to do this exercise. Ask yourself what would be the most frightening aspect of flying for you? It could be the moment of take-off or perhaps it's a fear of landing. Whichever it is, give it a maximum score of 100.

Now ask yourself which is the least frightening aspect of flying? This could be watching a plane fly overhead or looking at pictures of aeroplanes. Whatever it is, give it a score of just 5.

Now do this for all the situations in between, giving them an appropriate 'fear' score.

Example of how your sheet could look:

1.	Hearing an aeroplane in the distance	5
2.	Looking at aeroplanes in magazines	10
3.	Aeroplanes flying low over house	15
4.	Going to an aeroplane museum	20
5.	Looking at flight details in brochures	25
6.	Hearing about air disasters	30
7.	Discussing flights	35
8.	Visiting airports to collect people	40
9.	Booking a flight	45
10.	Realising day of flight has arrived	50
11.	Travelling to the airport	55
12.	Arriving at the airport	60
13.	Checking in at airport	65
14.	Waiting to board aircraft	70
15.	Walking down tunnel towards plane	75
16.	Walking down aisle towards seat	80
17.	Sitting, waiting for take-off	85
18.	Watching safety procedures	90
19.	Plane take-off	95
20.	Plane just about to land	100

You may well have other aspects of flying which you find more difficult, or perhaps you'd have things in a different order, so alter your list accordingly.

If your fear is of travelling on a motorway you can follow the same process. For example, you might give looking at a route map a score of 5 and overtaking in the outside lane a score of 100, with various situations in between scored appropriately. Take your time over compiling this exercise.

Lowering your anxiety reaction
Tackle each item on your list using the following steps:

1. Practise breathing and relaxation until you are calm and relaxed.

2. Relax all the body's muscle groups one at a time (from toes to head) until you feel totally relaxed.

3. Now let the first item of your list come into your mind for no more than 10 seconds. Visualise well and make it as clear as possible. Using the above list you would hear an aeroplane engine in the distance, gradually becoming louder and then quieter as it moves further away.

4. How tense are you feeling now?

5. Bring the first item to mind again and take a deep breath which you hold for a count of 5. Now let the breath out slowly whilst saying 'I am letting go'.

6. Now, notice how your tension has decreased, then remove the scene from your mind.

7. Repeat the above steps with the same scene again and notice how your anxiety levels have decreased even further.

8. Keep repeating this exercise with the same scene until you no longer feel anxious when imagining it.

Once you have done this, move on to your second fear, repeating all the above steps, and so on until each of the 20 points have been covered.

This exercise will need to be done over a period of time. But when you've finished, return to your original list and complete it again, noting how you've improved. Congratulations!

PLANNING YOUR JOURNEY

Travel, like an impromptu dinner party, is best planned as far ahead as possible. But in today's 'I want it by yesterday' world, planning isn't always possible. Much of your own travel will depend on your job and home life and the degree of flexibility they offer.

Before you set out on any journey – whether it's your daily run to work, school, the shops or whatever you need to ask yourself a few questions:

● Have I remembered everything (run through a list). *This can run from papers, money, clothes and telephone numbers to 'Have I switched off the immersion heater, gas cooker and hall light?'*

● Is there enough petrol in the car (if you're driving)? *If there isn't, have you brought enough money?*

● Am I timing this right (if you're using public transport or getting a lift)? *Have you checked timetables recently and whether your clocks are keeping good time?*

This may all seem like common sense, but it's amazing how many people admit to running through mental lists *after* they've left home, only to find they've forgotten something.

The advantages of not going out to work
The school run
If you don't work outside the home you *may* have a greater degree of flexibility than your working counterparts. But if you have school-age children who need lifts to and from school or other family commitments, then you will still have to keep to a fairly rigid timetable. One way around having to do this every day, sometimes twice a day, is to enlist the help of other parents. It makes good environmental and economic sense to use just one car daily to take the children to and from school. And it allows you to be free of the school run (and all its inevitable hassles) for up to four days a week.

Shopping
The joy of not working is that you can shop at quieter times, too, and avoid the mayhem of the Thursday or Friday night shop at your local supermarket.

Leisure
You can also travel to leisure activities during the day, when the traffic's quieter. Or you can walk or cycle and get yourself even fitter!

Working people
If you have no freedom about when you start or finish work, you'll probably have to travel at peak times and endure the rush hour with everyone else. But by accepting it as a vital part of your everyday routine and practising the points raised in this chapter you can lessen the impact it has on you. If you find the crowding on trains, underground or buses difficult to bear, imagine a glass dome coming over you. Let only positive energy through the dome and imagine it deflecting negative energy and pollution away like a shield.

Scan your body for tension at intervals, and mentally transcend your situation by practising the 'on the go' relaxation exercises discussed throughout this book.

Flexi-time
Many companies now offer their staff flexible working hours. This means you can start and finish work when you want (within reason!) and stagger your travel and lunch times. The benefit is that you can choose to travel outside of peak hours.

Using your car as an office

Invest in a mobile phone and if you sense you're going to be late for a meeting or sales appointment, pull off the road and ring in. This will immediately ease your mind and reduce your pressure load. You can also use it to keep in touch with friends and family when the day hasn't quite gone to plan, and you can ring customers and suppliers even when you're out of the office.

Keep a small filing system in your car with a duplicate of important telephone numbers and information you may need to hand. Carry a pen, clipboard and paper, or if you're into the latest technology, invest in a laptop computer complete with fax modem.

How about keeping a Dictaphone in the car too? When you next stop you can use it to dictate letters, notes or ideas which have come to you en route.

Working from home

With the advent of sophisticated technology, many people are able to do some or all of their job from home. This offers you even greater flexibility over travel arrangements. If you're not disciplined and self-motivated however, self-employment or home working may not be for you. Otherwise you'll only end up exchanging one set of pressures for another.

Visualisation

Visualisation is a useful tool to use when planning your journey. You can use it to 'script' how you would like the journey and day to go. On the morning of the journey (or the night before) visualise the journey you want. Make it as powerful and as realistic as possible. Imagine slipping into the driving seat or the train carriage. Smell the smells around you, hear the noises – the car's engine starting or the guard's whistle – and really 'buy into' the scene. Then go through your journey, 'programming' how you would like it to be. Even down to finding a parking space at the end of it, or a taxi waiting at the station with a lit 'For Hire' sign.

However you're travelling

Leave in plenty of time! If you need to leave by eight thirty, tell yourself you need to leave around eight if it's a local trip or even sooner if you're travelling long distance. By allowing extra time you won't feel at all pressured when all the traffic lights are against you, or you encounter a diversion a mile down the road. If you think back to some of the problems you've encountered on journeys, would they have been as bad if you'd allowed more time? Probably not.

ENTERTAINING YOURSELF EN ROUTE

Being realistic

Before you set off on your journey, ask yourself what you would do if you encountered a long hold-up. If you're travelling by train, aeroplane, coach or ferry, the answer may be different to the one you'd give if you've got to keep both hands firmly on a steering wheel. But however you're travelling, there's much you can do to entertain yourself – once you've practised your relaxation exercises of course!

Reading

One way to entertain yourself on a long journey or one fraught with hold-ups is to take a good book (or books) with you. Time seems to fly, too, when you are immersed in a good read. If you're one of those people who find it difficult to concentrate on books when in unfamiliar surroundings, take a magazine or two which you can dip into, and where most things are written in short 'bites'.

Listening

Even if you're driving, you can still 'read' by listening to talking books. There is a wide selection of audio books available which cater for all tastes and make ideal companions on a long journey. You don't always have to buy these as you can borrow them from your local library.

Alternatively you can listen to music. Throughout the ages the therapeutic value of music has been recognised and, surrounded by the right sounds, we can be invigorated and energised, soothed and balanced. Tapes of natural sounds can help reduce tension too, with waterfalls and crashing waves being popular choices. Classical music is pleasing, as are songs you can sing along with. Tunes with over 60 beats per minute have been shown to increase drivers' blood pressure, however, and make them uptight. So perhaps you should avoid music by Motorhead and Prodigy when driving and switch to something from Bach, Robbie Williams or the All Saints instead!

Avoid a diet of negativity when travelling, too. Choose to listen to interesting or amusing items on radio shows as further bad news when you're stuck in a three-mile tailback will not improve your tension levels.

And don't forget laughter. If you've got tapes of comedians or comedy shows, this is a great time to play them. Laughter is a wonderfully easy way to relieve tension.

Audio books, music and radio can all be played on personal stereos. But on some public transport they're banned, so make sure you're not flouting any laws when you play yours.

Learning

It's said that if you read for an hour a day on a chosen subject you could become an expert on it in a year. Yet another great reason for reading or listening to a language or study tape when travelling! Many self-improvement books are duplicated on audio tape now and you can choose from a wide selection including stress management, assertion and becoming a better communicator.

Business people have found travelling a great way of catching up on what's happening in the world of industry by listening to tapes on marketing and accounting. And they can now subscribe to a regular audio newsletter which contains a précis of new and current business and management titles. If you're a busy executive or manager this is an ideal way to keep in touch with innovative ideas in the business world. And if you like what you hear – go out and buy the book!

Relaxation

There are many audio tapes which will help you relax on your journey. But remember never to play deep relaxation programmes whilst driving or doing anything that requires your concentration. If you are a driver, however, there's nothing to stop you pulling over for a deep relaxation break. You'll restart the journey feeling much refreshed and in a better frame of mind. Alternatively, practise your 'relaxing on the go' exercise: regularly shrug and loosen your shoulders and stretch your legs when possible.

RE-ROUTING FOR PLEASURE

Is the route you take to work each day the same? And what about the way you travel to school, college or the shops? You've probably worked out which route is quickest and how long it takes and use it daily or weekly without giving alternatives much thought.

Taking a wrong turning

How many times do you pass a lane or junction and wonder what lies up there?

Next time, don't wonder, drive up it. You'll often be amazed at what you discover.

Or when you next go to the shops, try a different route. It will be much more interesting than the one you're familiar with. You'll see gardens which take your eye and give you ideas for your own, and pass dry cleaners and carpet shops you didn't even know existed. Even if you encounter hold-ups on your new route, you'll have new shop windows to look at and different people to watch.

Visiting familiar haunts
When you're planning to visit friends or family again, consider a different form of transport. If you usually drive, catch a coach or a train. Let someone else take the strain while you spend the journey reading, relaxing and observing your fellow passengers!

Travelling to somewhere new

If you're driving somewhere for the first time, it's worthwhile asking friends and colleagues if they've done the journey before. If so, they can give you tips to make the trip more enjoyable, such as altering your route to avoid rush-hour bottlenecks and contra flow systems. They'll be able to tell you which cafés offer the best food or suggest pleasant stopping places if you're taking your own lunch.

Try not to have preconceived ideas about the place you're visiting. Make up your own mind when you get there and don't allow yourself to be influenced by others. People often associate places with events. If they had a horrid time there with their ex-husband, for example, it may well colour their judgement.

Enjoying the time

Make a pact with yourself to enjoy travel. Recognise it as a necessary part of your everyday life, whether it's on foot, by bicycle or in the driving seat.

Consider:

● using an alternative form of transport

● travelling at different times

● using a different route.

Remember to:

● plan ahead

● be realistic about the possibility of hold-ups and delays

● take a book, magazine, tape or some form of 'entertainment'

  (*particularly important if you have children with you*).

Practise:

- visualisation

- relaxation

- overcoming fears.

Using the tools we have discussed in this chapter you can improve all your journeys. Bon voyage!

CASE STUDY

Julia battles with the crowds

Every Thursday evening Julia battled with trolleys and crowds at her local supermarket, in much the same way as she drove to school every morning when other parents were doing the same thing at the same time!

As Julia worked at home, the school run wasn't a good start to the day. She would arrive back home irritated and tense, which did nothing to put her in a good frame of mind for working.

'Why do you do things you find so stressful?' a friend asked.

'Because I have to,' was the reply.

On reflection, Julia realised she didn't have to. There were alternatives – so she pursued them. Putting a notice in the school newsletter bought a flood of replies from willing parents only too happy to share in taking the children to and from school. Now Julia drives the children to school only one day out of every seven. Because it's such a novelty, she quite enjoys the day she does, knowing that the following day it will be someone else's responsibility. And guess what? Julia now uses one of her 'spare' mornings to shop at the local supermarket when it's quiet.

KEY POINTS

- View travel differently – it's not what happens that matters, it's how you react to it.

- Plan to be flexible – consider every alternative.

- Educate, amuse and entertain yourself en route.

- Regularly scan your body for tension before, during and after a journey.

- Use visualisation before setting off, however long or short the trip.

ACTIVITY

Think of a place you regularly travel to which is three or more miles away. It may be your workplace, college, friend's or relative's house, supermarket, garage, school or garden centre.

1. Using a map, work out five different ways of getting there and label them 1, 2, 3, 4 and 5.

2. Compare these to your normal route and approximate how much more (or less) time each route will take.

3. Now use each of these routes in turn for the next five times you make the journey.

Make sure you allow at least 20 minutes longer for each journey than you anticipate to allow for hold-ups, etc. When you've done each journey consider the new things you've noticed. Did it take more or less time than you thought? Did you find the variety made the journey less tedious? Why not choose another of your regular destinations and do the same thing all over again?

8

Activities for Relaxation

In order for us to gain a balanced, relaxed way of life we need activity – both physical and mental. We need to keep our bodies and minds in good shape.

Getting yourself into shape is a great stress buster. And as you get fitter, you'll notice your life getting better. That's because your health will improve along with your outlook, and you'll gain more confidence.

Your body is designed to be active, and the popular saying *use it or lose it* has a great ring of truth about it!

BENEFITS OF PHYSICAL EXERCISE

Would you like to:

● improve your sleep?

● have fewer headaches?

● experience fewer stress-related aches and pains?

● achieve a greater sense of inner peace and tranquillity?

● improve your mental clarity and concentration?

● have greater physical stamina?

Most people would, and you can, simply by taking regular exercise. That's because the above are just some of the benefits reported by people who enjoy regular exercise of one form or another.

Nowadays, we do far less physically than our bodies were designed to, so exercise is important. Not only will it have a tremendous effect on your circulation, breathing and other body processes, it will also have an immediate, positive effect on your emotions, anxieties and worries. Being physically fit is an advantage too, when attempting to meet the physical and emotional challenges life presents you with.

It is recognised that people who are physically fit are psychologically fit. A doctor at the University of Virginia says that neither he nor his colleagues have ever treated a physically-fit depressed person. And many studies have shown how people have greatly improved their state of mind simply by raising their physical fitness levels.

Good economics
Think of the time you invest in your home, your car, your job, your family. Doesn't it make sense to invest in yourself too? Putting aside regular time to exercise also makes excellent economic sense, since the fitter you are the better your decisions will be and the less likely you are to suffer from a stress-related illness. You'll take fewer days off work, and, as you become more resistant to illnesses and infections, you'll spend less money on over-the-counter remedies and prescriptions.

Body changes
Climbers, runners and others who exercise regularly say they experience a much greater sense of calm within their lives, often developing a greater awareness of their own spirituality. It can also help you to take a step back from your life and to view it and events with greater equanimity.

Energetic physical exercise not only works off the effects of stress but helps to limit it by triggering the production of powerful brain chemicals which induce feelings of happiness and kill pain. Exercise stimulates your circulation and your vital organs, improves your breathing function and has the advantage of reducing tension in your muscles. So, the next time you have a particularly tough day at home or work, take some vigorous exercise, and notice how different you feel. It's almost impossible to remain angry or frustrated when exercising, and afterwards you will have more energy, feel calmer and be able to spend a far more relaxed evening.

Are you fit enough to exercise?
This may sound like a silly question as taking physical exercise will undoubtedly make you fitter! But if you currently have or have had a health problem please check with your doctor first to see which form of exercise they recommend. Even if you've got restricted movement, don't despair, exercise can take many forms as you'll see later in this chapter.

Fitness tests
The following tests are a way of gauging your current level of fitness. But you must stop immediately if you experience discomfort in your chest, pain, shortness of breath or start to feel sick, dizzy or winded.

Resting pulse
A quick and general way of checking your level of fitness is by taking your pulse rate when you are resting. Are you within the 'normal' range shown below?

70–85 beats per minute for men

75–90 beats per minute for women

If you are unfit when you start exercising, your pulse rate will increase rapidly and take much longer to return to normal than for someone who is fit. If you are fit, however, you will start with a low pulse rate, have it stay lower during exercise and notice it quickly return to normal when you stop.

People who exercise regularly and are considered fit have a consistently lower pulse rate than those who are unfit. Ideally, during exercise you need to achieve and maintain an optimum pulse rate to gain maximum benefit. One formula suggests working out your optimum pulse rate by deducting your age from 220 and multiplying the result by three and then dividing it by four – the answer is the target pulse rate to aim for during exercise. But remember never to exceed this.

Strength
To test your arm, shoulder and chest muscles try the following press-ups while keeping your legs completely straight:

1. Stand 1m away from a desk or table.

2. Place your hands on the table and bring your chest down to meet the desk edge.

3. Now lift yourself away from the table.

4. Repeat.

How many did you manage? If you managed to do up to eight or ten, this is good; between four and seven is average, and less than that is poor.

To test your stomach muscles, lie flat on your back with your arms folded. Now try and roll yourself up into a sitting position. If you can't do it then your strength in that region is extremely poor. If you can get halfway up then that's fairly average. But if you can sit up and repeatedly do this exercise you can consider yourself to have good strength in your abdomen.

Endurance

One way of testing your endurance is to run on the spot, lifting your knees high while keeping your breathing to a regular (not gasping) level. If you can do so for over two minutes that's good; less than one minute is poor, with anything between being average.

Are you flexible?

Sit on the floor with your legs stretched out straight in front of you, keeping them together. Can your reach your toes? Yes? Then your flexibility is good. If you can just about reach your ankles then that's fairly average. If not, your flexibility is poor.

You are probably already aware of your current fitness levels and recognise where your strengths and weaknesses lie. Now all you have to do is get active and choose which activities and exercises are right for you.

FINDING EXERCISE WHICH SUITS YOU

There are numerous ways you can exercise. Many people choose a combination which suits their location, their age and current levels of fitness. You may choose to swim once or twice a week and walk every day. That's because you need to take physical exercise for at least ten minutes every day. But if this really isn't possible, then exercise four times a week for at least 20 minutes at a time.

If you're reluctant to take up exercise, take heart, for many people have felt that way. But having initially forced themselves to take regular exercise, they now report that it's one of the most enjoyable things they do!

Exercising choice

There are many things you may want to ask yourself before choosing which form of exercise is best for you. Questions such as:

- How much time are you prepared to devote to exercising?

- At what time or times of the day can you exercise?

- Do you want to do it alone or with friends?

- Do you want to join a formal class?

- Do you want to do the same exercise or do you want to try different things?

And, depending upon which exercise you choose, how much cost is involved?

Answering these questions will help you decide which form of exercise to try first. After all, you can always change if you find it doesn't suit you. But that's not the same as giving up – perseverance is the key!

Popular forms of exercise

Swimming
Most towns have swimming pools and if you have the flexibility to go at quiet times – so much the better. If you live near the sea, this can be an option, but often the weather makes this prohibitive for all but the most dedicated of sea swimmers. Swimming is a great way to improve your heart, lungs, joints and muscles. And by using different strokes you can give different muscles a good workout. Try swimming for up to half an hour without stopping.

Many towns now have hydrotherapy pools where the water temperature is constantly kept higher for people with health and mobility problems. Contact your local pool for more details.

Cycling
With the advent of exercise cycles you don't even need to leave home to cycle. But cycling outdoors has additional benefits. You will have an opportunity to breathe fresh air (depending on where you cycle!) and see things you wouldn't normally notice when driving in the car. You'll meet people too at a speed which allows you to acknowledge them, so overall it's more enjoyable than using an exercise bike.

Running
You can run almost anywhere. Inside, outside, on a track or in a field; up and down your garden or around the house. The weather will often determine where you run as ploughing through a muddy field may not be much fun. Running is a good form of exercise for those of you who wish to be alone, although you can run in groups or with partners. Wear good supportive shoes wherever you run, and stop immediately if you experience pain.

Dancing
Dancing is often overlooked as a form of exercise. But if you like music, few activities are as enjoyable. Although considered to be something you do with a partner or in a group, it is possible to dance alone in the

privacy of your own home. Put on your favourite records and dance non-stop for ten minutes or more. The choice of dance is yours, and you can vary it to suit your taste and moods. Boogie to disco beats or waltz, quickstep or foxtrot to the strains of your favourite orchestra. Weekly line dancing sessions are being held in village halls and town centres up and down the country and are great social occasions as well as an excellent way of getting fit.

Keep fit
Keep fit classes are another popular way of exercising either in a group or on your own. There are many videos and cassettes on sale which you can use at home to help you follow a set programme of exercises to improve your strength and mobility. Generally however, keep fit classes are a great way of meeting other people and receiving instruction from a qualified teacher. Wear loose clothing or stretchy exercise leggings and leotards.

Restricted movement
If you've got limited or restricted movement in some joints or muscles, you can still enjoy exercising other areas of your body. Simple stretching movements or 'jogging' in a chair using only your arms for 15 minutes can improve your heart and breathing function. Ask your doctor, physiotherapist or other health professional about other forms of exercise you can follow. And remember, you don't need to be able bodied to abseil, play netball or complete a marathon these days – but you will need determination.

PUTTING YOUR BEST FOOT FORWARD
One of the most overlooked forms of exercise is walking, which is excellent for your heart, lungs, back, circulation and overall sense of well-being. Get into the habit of walking by laying down rules for yourself. Rule one could be that you never drive less than a mile. Rule two could be that you refuse to use a lift when you can use stairs.

When walking to get fit you need to:

1. walk briskly *and*

2. take long strides which cause you to breathe deeply.

Try and do this for 20 minutes without stopping, then increase it to half an hour, three or four times a week if possible.

The joy of exercising in this way is that it can literally be done anywhere at any time. But remember, exercising in the fresh air is always preferential to exercising indoors, so whenever you can, get out and walk. Adjust the pace to your level of fitness and don't make excuses not to do so. If it's raining, pull on a raincoat or grab an umbrella. And if your destination is so far away you really must take your car – park further way than you normally would – and walk that final mile!

AVOIDING ADDITIONAL PRESSURE

When considering a form of exercise you may think of squash, badminton, rugby, netball or similar sport. But if you already lead a pressured lifestyle avoid taking up a competitive sport such as these. Otherwise you'll only succeed in placing yourself under additional strain and pressure.

Most of all, exercise needs to be fun. Do something you enjoy so it doesn't become just another pressure in your life. And don't overlook the obvious things like singing (great for breathing and exercising the lungs), dancing and walking. Your objective is to get fit.

Gently does it
Although it's commendable that you've decided to start exercising, do things gradually to avoid straining or exhausting yourself. You need to build up your fitness programme over a period of time. If you've been driving everywhere for the past 20 years, you're certainly not going to be able to run several miles at your first attempt. Improve your stamina by gently increasing the distance and speed at which you run. The same is true of whichever form of exercise you choose.

Enjoyment factor
You are far less likely to stick at an activity which you don't enjoy, so don't take up rowing if you don't enjoy being on the water. Look instead at something you enjoy or feel you could grow to enjoy. If you like listening to music, consider dancing, keep fit or aerobics. If you want to be part of a group, attend regular classes or ask a friend to get fit with you – anything which makes the prospect of exercise fun.

Remember, however, that taking regular exercise puts you on a positive spiral – the more you do, the fitter you become and the more you'll enjoy life. So persevere, it's worth it.

Making excuses

How many times have you agreed to something in the morning which you regret by the end of the day? It's the same with exercise. You start off with great intentions about going for a half an hour run in the evening. By the time you've had supper, sat in the armchair, watched a bit of TV and had a doze, the last thing you want to do is drag yourself out for an evening run. So make your exercise convenient. Exercise on the way home from work if possible, or set the alarm and get up earlier.

Exercising with a friend is another good way of avoiding excuses. You have to go because they're waiting for you. And you can't let them down, can you?

Varying your routine

The benefits of adding variety to your exercise regime are twofold. Not only will it aid different muscle groups and body systems it will also prevent you from becoming bored with one activity. You may wish to walk one time, cycle the next, and swim another. Alternating activities this way helps keep you motivated too.

If you really enjoy one activity, you can add variety to that. If you cycle, walk or run, for instance, try different routes.

SELECTING LEISURE PURSUITS

We need mental stimulation too. Hobbies, pastimes, something that holds our interest and takes us out of ourselves every so soften.

Relaxing hobbies

As well as stimulating our mental processes, creative hobbies can help us unwind. They can help soothe us when life gets fraught and give our minds a rest from everyday concerns.

Gardening

If you enjoy gardening you already know how relaxing it can be. Pottering about amongst the plants and shrubs, pruning, deadheading and pricking out seeds. The joy of gardening is that it can be both a relaxing hobby and a good form of exercise (such as when you're mowing the lawn). But don't forget to spend some time just sitting idly and being. Gardens are perfect for this. Include a seat in your garden, next to scented plants perhaps and a trickle of water. Now relax.

Creative hobbies

The hobby you choose will depend on your personal preferences, but could include model-making, painting or writing. But don't make a chore out of your hobby by becoming a perfectionist. If you've never painted but want to give it a go – do so. If you've enjoyed creating a watercolour, pastel or oil painting, that's great, even if the result isn't something you'd expect to see in the Louvre. Besides, you can only get better!

Writing can take many forms. You may wish to keep a journal for personal use, or one that you can hand on to your children when they're older. Perhaps you enjoy writing letters or short stories. Is there a book in you dying to get out? Start writing today. If you're concerned about spelling, punctuation, style – don't be. Just write. You can always attend a class later to help you get it into a publishable form.

Making time

Wherever your interests lie you can find time to pursue them. It may mean rising earlier, going to bed later or spending less time in front of the TV or with your friends, but you can do it. Refer back to the sections on time management (Chapter 4) to see how!

CASE STUDY

Billy surprises himself

Billy was approaching 50. He was slightly overweight, drove everywhere, was a bit of a worrier and had an appalling diet. He was always talking about taking more exercise, but never did anything about it. He couldn't even be bothered to walk to the newsagent in the morning for a paper.

When a colleague at work developed serious health problems, Billy began to worry. They were about the same age and their lifestyles were almost identical. After getting himself checked out at the doctor's, Billy took up running. At first, he had real problems getting out of bed early. He dreaded the mornings he'd set aside to do so, but still forced himself to get up and go.

After a month or so, Billy found the running getting easier and he was able to go further. He began to notice too, that on the mornings he felt a bit depressed, the feelings would go almost as soon as he started running. He always returned much happier. Looking back, Billy can now see it was a turning point in his life. His diet's improved, his health has improved, and colleagues have commented on how positive he's become. So much so, he's organised a company Fun Run in aid of a local children's charity.

KEY POINTS

- Bodies are designed to be active.

- Walking is a great form of exercise. It's free and can be done almost anywhere, anytime.

- If you are not used to strenuous exercise check your fitness before you start.

- People who exercise regularly limit their chances of stress, and work off the effects of it too.

- If you already lead a pressured lifestyle avoid taking up a competitive sport.

- Make time for a relaxing hobby to give your mind a rest from everyday concerns from time to time.

ACTIVITY

Choose a form of exercise, such as running, dancing or cycling, for example. On Monday morning rise earlier than normal and spend five minutes exercising. If, when you wake on Monday morning, you feel as if it's the last thing you want to do – do it anyway! Force yourself.

On Wednesday morning, again rise earlier and spend five minutes exercising. On Friday morning do the same.

Repeat this the following week, only this time increase the exercise period to ten minutes per session. And on week three increase it to 15 minutes.

Keep a log during the three weeks detailing how you feel emotionally and physically. Are you more positive, for instance? Do you find yourself getting angered less? Are you eating more healthily? Are you sleeping better? The answers will invariably be 'yes'. And, like most people, you will discover that the exercise you once avoided as a chore has become an enjoyable part of your life. Something you actually look forward to!

9

Becoming a Relaxed Person

Using relaxation for health and success hinges on many things – your diet, exercise, relaxation techniques, managing your time effectively, and all the other things talked about in this book. You may choose to improve upon one aspect of your lifestyle, such as diet. You will certainly benefit from doing so – but not in the way you would if you embraced *all* the aspects of living a more relaxed life. The 'tools' are all interconnected, one impacting upon the other, and so on. So introduce them all into your lifestyle, gradually if necessary. Not only will you feel happier, you'll look better too, with less frown lines, brighter eyes and fewer skin problems or aches and pains. Yes, relaxation does wonders for your physical appearance too.

REMOVING PROPS

When your life isn't going well or you're not feeling too happy about yourself you may prop it up with something without even realising it. Props can take many forms, but once you recognise them as just that, you can choose to cut them out.

Comfort food

When you shop do you notice how you're drawn to different things according to how you feel? If your life is going well and you feel good about yourself, your shopping trolley will contain lots of fresh fruit and vegetables and other healthy foods. If you don't feel quite so good about yourself and your life, it's likely you'll reach out for 'comfort' foods. These are usually things like sugar-rich snacks and sugary foods. Eating large quantities of sugary foods may lead to low blood sugar (hypoglycaemia) which can cause fatigue and irritability – and so the cycle continues.

Notice, too, when you start munching 'comfort' foods. Is it when you're on the telephone, or feeling bored? If so, break the pattern.

Nicotine

Smoking cigarettes causes major health problems, even death, yet many people still choose to continue. It is generally accepted that giving up cigarettes is difficult because they are habit-forming, but it is not impossible. Many ex-smokers now recognise that giving up was difficult or almost impossible when their life wasn't how they wanted it to be. In other words, the cigarettes were a prop. But once they felt happier about themselves and their lifestyle – giving up was much easier.

Caffeine

Tea and coffee, like many other things, are acceptable in moderation. But if you find yourself reaching out for either to help you through your day, then you're using it as a prop. Caffeine is stress-inducing and can cause a variety of health problems, so try one of the many herbal teas as an alternative, or drink water or fruit juice.

Alcohol

In moderation, alcohol isn't all bad. Drinking is often a way of socialising and relaxing with family, friends or colleagues. Excess alcohol doesn't really make you relax though – it's a depressant. So, if you find yourself needing to have a drink to face something or someone, or you're unable to go on without a drink, or you're concealing the amount you drink from those around you – alcohol is your prop and you need to do something fast. Ask yourself:

1. Why do you drink?
   - *For instance, are you unhappy, bored. angry, self-loathing?*
2. How could you cut down on your drinking?
   - *Avoid seeing certain people?*
   - *Avoid going to certain places?*
   - *Spend more time on activities/hobbies/exercise?*

Alcohol, like nicotine, is addictive, so it will require determination on your part to reduce or cut it out. You may even need help from your doctor, or other professional to achieve a better quality of life. Do whatever it takes.

Medication

There are times in all our lives when we need medical attention. And part of that attention may involve being prescribed painkillers, sleeping tablets or other medicine. In the short term these may be useful, even necessary. In the longer term, unless you have a chronic condition, they are far less useful, and may be damaging.

If you have a headache, consider alternatives before reaching for painkillers – relaxation, massage, aromatherapy or a short nap. Later, consider what caused the headache. Was it lack of sleep? Tension? Pent-up frustration? If so, try and deal with the root cause instead of taking pills that will only mask the symptoms of an undesirable lifestyle.

LIVING POSITIVELY

Living positively is a wonderful way to live. It isn't about pretending that things or people don't upset you when they do. Or keeping sadness and other emotions locked inside. It's choosing to think, act, react and speak positively.

Most of us say the things we do and act a certain way out of habit. Think of a situation or person that always manages to irritate you. Think of the past few times this has happened. Do you see a pattern emerging? They say this and you say that and before you know it you've had the same disagreement all over again. Make a pact with yourself to react differently next time – refuse to get angry, for instance, or agree to differ.

A positive loop
Positivity is like a loop – what you give out you get back. Has anyone given you positive encouragement in your life? Yes? Then you'll know just how good it feels to have someone believe in you. You make a special effort, put everything into a project because someone believes in you. Now think of someone who is always negative. Just thinking of someone like this can make you feel tired and 'low'. They constantly say, 'If only …', focus on the bleaker side of situations, and condemn and blame others. Naturally, someone like this won't attract positive people into their lives. Sadly, this just serves to reinforce the negative view they have of the world.

Positivity and health
There have been numerous studies done which prove the link between good health and positivity. And, as one famous physician put it, 'All the vitamin C in the world won't make up for a lousy attitude'. Our minds and bodies are unquestionably linked. We cannot possibly make a change in one without affecting the other.

For instance:

●   stand up straight, with your shoulders back

●   look upwards towards the ceiling and smile.

Do you feel depressed? No, it's impossible to feel depressed without changing your physical posture! To actually experience the emotion of depression, you not only have to focus your thoughts on sadness, you have to assume a depressive posture – slumped, round shouldered, shallow breathing, looking downwards, mouth set. That's because our physiology affects our emotions and thought processes, and our thought processes and emotions affect our physiology.

In knowing this you can choose not to feel depressed.

Positive challenge
Refuse to let a single negative thought enter your head for 24 hours if it does, say to yourself, *'I delete that thought'*, then replace it with a positive one. You may be amazed at just how many negative thoughts you usually have. So, if someone is late picking you up for instance, don't complain, tell yourself you've been given a gift of time! Once you've mastered this for a complete 24 hours, congratulate yourself and increase the challenge to 48 hours!

RELAXING MIND AND BODY

Every once in a while, you need to 'shut off'. Not to have to think about working, shopping, ironing, bills, relationships, gardening, families, deadlines, children, parents, what's right and what's wrong. If you instinctively feel you'd like to do this – you're right. Your mind and body is telling you that it wants a break, and if you're being sensible, you'll heed the request.

Resilience
Your body is remarkable in the way it keeps going, despite the fact you may not always feed it or rest it properly. It's the same with your mind – it carries on regardless. But stress is cumulative.

When young, most of us can cope with much emotional and physical pressure. Other factors will influence how well we cope, of course, including how we see others around us coping, our diet, the amount of exercise we take and so on. But often as we go through life, our ability to deal with stress lessens. We may not have dealt with earlier problems and challenges either, which means that new pressures are piled on top of the old ones, and so the pressures grow.

Respite

It's clear that we all need a break from everyday life – both physically and emotionally. Imagine you're like the 'volcano' in Figure 3. At the bottom lie the unresolved problems you've battled with throughout your life – lack of self-esteem and confidence; regret over losing a loved one to someone else, problems in childhood, bitterness, perhaps, that seemingly less deserving people have had better luck in their life.

The middle layer may be the challenges you're facing on a day-to-day basis – money concerns, unsatisfying relationships, ageing parents in failing health, housing problems or similar. You'll see then that it doesn't take too much to cause the small top layer of your 'volcano' to erupt, when something relatively minor happens – such as a dog getting under your feet or a partner or child asking you for some extra money.

If you don't resolve the underlying issues these relatively unimportant things will cause you to flare up and erupt almost constantly. It's essential therefore to give yourself a gift of time. Time to consider and resolve issues that may have held you back in the past and created unnecessary pressures in your life. It is possible to take time out of your normal routine. It may mean asking for help and take much organising – ringing around, writing and networking, but you can do it.

BEING YOURSELF IN RELATIONSHIPS

You have relationships with many groups of people. Friends, family, parents, children, colleagues, bosses, employees, shop assistants, in fact everyone you encounter in your life. Some relationships may be short whilst others continue for a lifetime.

Quality not quantity

One-off meetings

Have you ever met a person just once, yet found they had a profound effect on your life? Perhaps it was something they said or did which touched you in an unforgettable way. It may have been a brave act or simply a single word – the length of their involvement isn't important, it was the quality of their involvement with you that mattered.

1.   Think about the relationships you have with others.

2.   Would you term them quality or quantity relationships? They can be both.

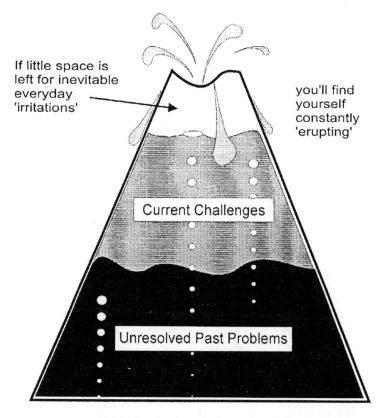

If little space is left for inevitable everyday 'irritations'

you'll find yourself constantly 'erupting'

Current Challenges

Unresolved Past Problems

Fig. 3. Are you 'erupting' unnecessarily?

Friends

Many people have lots of friends, but no one they feel comfortable confiding in. Is this you? You cannot be all things to all people, so it's naive to think that all your friends can be too. But it's important to foster relationships with people you can confide in when necessary, and share your successes with too. And the easiest way of doing this is by being a true friend yourself.

Colleagues

Is the *core* of you the same whether you're at work or at home, or do you change within each role? Consistency is one of the qualities we look for in others and one of the things we can offer in all our relationships. Have you ever come across someone who is quiet and unassuming at home, but who then turns into a dictator in the workplace? Some people imagine that to lead or manage people this is necessary, but that is not so.

List the qualities of managers and leaders you respect. Bullying, inconsistency and humiliation will not be on the list.

So, who are you?

Are you your *true* self in relationships? If not, who are you? Someone you think your partner, wife or husband will prefer? Someone you think friends will want to be with or colleagues will look up to? If so, it's likely you're placing a lot of unnecessary pressure on yourself by being who you think others want you to be instead of being who you really are. Is this because you lack confidence or don't value yourself enough?

It's natural to want people to think the best of you, especially when meeting them for the first time, but don't act or pretend to be someone you're not.

If you don't rate yourself very highly, it's unlikely others will either, so begin to do something about that today.

Using affirmations
A simple first step is to start saying and writing affirmations daily. Positive, personal statements such as:

● I accept myself completely.

● I deserve and accept the best life has to offer.

● New opportunities are presenting themselves to me.

● I love who I am and what I do.

● Something wonderful is happening to me today.

Make up some of your own, ensuring that they are positive and in the present. Don't postpone your development by saying 'New opportunities *will* present themselves to me' – talk as if they already are presenting themselves!

Put aside some time to write your chosen affirmations over and over again, as many times as you've got time for. It helps to reinforce the messages.

Becoming someone you want to be
If you know you have undesirable traits – work on them. One at a time if necessary. But remember you are human and humans make mistakes – thankfully.

SAYING 'YES' TO HEALTHY PRESSURE

When did you last rise to a challenge? Was it yesterday when you returned a faulty lamp to the store although your heart was thumping and you felt light-headed at the prospect? Or was it when you flew across the Atlantic despite a long-standing fear of flying? Whatever challenge you confronted, congratulate yourself.

What is a challenge? The answer is that it varies from person to person. What you might take in your stride, your neighbour might consider a major challenge, and vice versa. You may be at ease speaking in public, while most other people say they would rather die first. Perhaps you are terrified at the prospect of holding a snake, or cooking for 30. Others may love the idea.

Moving beyond comfort
If you never do anything except the things you feel comfortable with, your life will never hold any more than it does now. And you will never move beyond your comfort zone. As a result you will never experience the tremendous thrills and 'highs' which can only come from finally conquering something which, for you, has been a personal challenge. it takes courage, but being courageous is doing things in spite of all the reasons why you thought you couldn't.

● it's speaking in public *despite* feeling as if you're going to faint

● it's abseiling down a cliff face *despite* being terrified of heights

● it's joining a local group *despite* having palpitations at the thought of meeting new people

● it's booking up driving lessons *despite* feeling ill when you think of it

● it's doing things *in spite of* ...

And never assume life is more difficult for you than for anybody else – everyone has their own set of challenges to overcome.

So saying 'Yes' to challenges generates healthy pressure. Along with this come feelings of self-worth and achievement. Yes! Taking control of your life and what it holds is what you do when you value yourself.

ADOPTING CALM CHARACTERISTICS

Have you ever been in a room, office, shop or classroom when someone has rushed in, obviously irritated, dashed around snatching at things they wanted and raced out again? They probably left you feeling tense as if it was you who'd been rushing and irritated.

Some people, however, have the ability to make you feel relaxed and balanced. Their presence is calming, relaxing, soothing and you soon find yourself feeling less tense, less hurried and less agitated.

You, too, can become more relaxed and have a calming influence on others by adopting the characteristics of someone who is calm and relaxed.

Try:

1. talking more slowly

2. keeping an even tone when talking

3. not raising your voice too high

4. moving more slowly

5. avoiding sharp cutting movements with you hands

6. not drumming your fingers

7. eating more slowly

8. chewing your food for longer

9. holding your head level when conversing

10. dropping your shoulders

11. breathing slowly and rhythmically.

These are just some of the characteristics of a calm person. One by one you can adopt them. And by acting calm, you will become calm.

And finally ...
You now have the tools to help you become a relaxed person. In six months from now, if you follow the recommendations in this book, you will notice changes in yourself. Some will be dramatic, others more subtle, but changes nevertheless. Nothing stays the same no matter how much you may want it to. With every passing second, life alters. Accept that change is inevitable, embrace it, grow with the changes and lead a successful and healthy life.

CASE STUDY
Paul stays awake worrying
Paul felt sick on the morning of the relaxation course. His head was

throbbing, he felt dizzy and was tempted to ring the college to say he couldn't go. He always felt like this when he was expected to go somewhere different and meet new people. He knew his behaviour had a negative effect on the whole family. They never attended parties, or went out to dinner, or other social events because every time they were due to go anywhere his symptoms would return. And his problem had prevented them taking the children on a proper holiday for years. Last night his wife had given him an ultimatum – either he confronted his fear and went to the class regardless or she was moving out and taking the children with her.

Getting to the college that morning was a blur, and Paul was sure he would faint if he was asked to answer anything in front of the others. But the tutor was friendly and seemed to recognise he was nervous. The morning passed quickly and during the break he learned that many others had spent sleepless nights worrying about going to classes too. Paul felt a different person as he drove home – quite elated. It was the first time he'd forced himself to do something despite feeling so terrible and he was glad he had. He'd survived! And he knew instinctively that he'd taken the first step towards changing his and his family's life for the better.

KEY POINTS

● Look out for the 'props' in your life which prevent you from dealing with the underlying issues.

● Stress is cumulative.

● Your mind and body are unquestionably linked, you cannot make a change in one without affecting the other.

● You can choose to think, act, react and speak positively.

● Learn how to be yourself, not who you think others want you to be.

ACTIVITY

Write down your answers to the following questions.

1. Name something you are going to change *today* as a result of reading this book.

2. Which characteristics do you most admire in others?

3. Which of the above characteristics do you possess?

4. Which area of your life do you recognise you need to work on most?

Now you need to *act* on your answers to questions 1 to 4. The first question asked you what you were going to do today as a result of reading this book. Perhaps your answer was to relax more, make a *Not To Do* list, go for a swim or apply for a job you have always wanted. Whatever it is, you must do something towards it today!

What about your answers to questions 2 and 3? Do you already possess the qualities you admire most in others? Perhaps you admire patient people who are assertive. If you would like to be more assertive, book yourself on a course. If you would like to be more patient – then practise. Remain calm when watching others do things you know you can do quicker, and if you find yourself in a long queue simply drop your shoulders, smile and be patient.

Now that you recognise which areas of your life you need to work on most, you need to go ahead and do it. Don't delay. If you fail to reflect and act upon your answers nothing will change for you. But if you have absorbed the messages throughout this book and acted upon the guidelines and activities, you will soon be feeling a different person – if you're not already.

Glossary

Affirmations. Personal positive statements which you write or repeat to yourself.

Alpha. A wave emitted by your brain when you are deeply relaxed.

Aromatherapy. Massage of essential oils into the skin – oils obtained from a wide variety of flowers, plants and trees which can stimulate, soothe or heal according to type. The aroma of essential oils can also be inhaled.

Beta. Brain wave emitted when you are awake.

Challenge. Something which requires you to go beyond your comfort zone.

Comfort zone. Those areas of your life which you feel comfortable being in.

Delta. Wave emitted by your brain when you sleep and dream.

Fight or flight. The response your body produces automatically when confronted with what it perceives to be a threat.

Ions. Electrically charged negative and positive particles in the atmosphere.

Ioniser. A device which outputs healthy negative ions to keep the air in your home fresh and clear.

Massage. Stroking, kneading and rubbing movements, using warm massage oil, to help relax tense muscles and improve blood circulation.

Meditation. Achieving inner stillness and relaxation by a combination of breathing exercises and focusing the mind on a single object, word or thought.

Reframing. Looking at things in a different way.

Relaxation. Relieving your body of external stimuli.

Relaxation response. When you're fully relaxed (opposite of the fight or flight response).

Self-esteem. To have value, or self-respect, for oneself.

Stress-proofing. Plans to limit excessive pressure.

Theta. Brain wave emitted when you're sleepy.

Time management. Managing your time productively to make the best use of every day.

Visualisation. Going through a situation in the mind, step by step, and overturning negative aspects by visualising positive outcomes.

Yoga. A Hindu religious system of meditation, the first stages of which, also known as hatha yoga, have become popular in the West as a form of exercise and relaxation. These stages involve self-discipline, physical preparation, breathing exercises and meditation.

Useful Addresses

Air Quality Helpline, Tel: (0800) 556677.

Amaravati Buddhist Monastery, Great Gaddesden, Hemel Hempstead, Herts HP1 3BZ. Tel: (0144) 284 2455 (Amaravati Monastery also runs a programme of guided meditation retreats suitable for beginners, write for details).

Aromatherapy Organisations Council, 3 Latymer Close, Braybrooke, Market Harborough, Leics LE16 8LN. Tel: (01858) 434242.

Association of Reflexologists, 27 Old Gloucester Street, London WC1N 3XX. Tel: (0990) 673320.

British Acupuncture Council, Park House, 206–208 Latimer Road, London W10 6RE. Tel: (0181) 964 0222.

British Association for Counselling, 1 Regents Place, Rugby CV2 2PJ. Tel: (01788) 578328.

British Massage Therapy Council, Greenbank House, 65a Adelphi Street, Preston, Lancs PR1 7BH. Tel: (01772) 881063.

Chithurst Buddhist Monastery, Chithurst, Petersfield, Hants GU31 5EU. Tel: (01730) 814986.

Cranio-Sacral Therapy Association, Monomark House, 27 Old Gloucester Street, London WC1N 3XX. Tel: (0181) 543 4969.

Dr Edward Bach Centre, Mount Vernon, Sotwell, Wallingford, Oxon OX10 0PZ. Tel: (01491) 834678.

Drinkline, Tel: (0345) 320202.

Hartridge Buddhist Monastery, Upottery, Honiton, Devon EX14 5EU. Tel: (01404) 891251 (write for details of beginners' meditation workshops).

National Institute of Medical Herbalists, 56 Longbrook Street, Exeter, Devon EX4 6AH. Tel: (01392) 426022.

National Register of Hypnotherapists and Psychotherapists, 12 Cross Street, Nelson, Lancs BB9 7EN. Tel: (01282) 699378.

Quitline (for smoking), Tel: (0800) 002200.

Reiki Association, Cornbrook Bridge House, Clee Hill, Ludlow, Salop SY8 3QQ. Tel: (01981) 550829.

SAD Association, PO Box 989, Steyning BN33 3HG.

Samaritans, Tel: (0345) 909090.

Saneline, Tel: (0345) 678000.

Shiatsu Society, 5 Foxcote, Wokingham, Berks RG11 3PG. Tel: (01483) 860771.

Society of Homeopaths, 2 Artisan Road, Northampton NN1 4HU. Tel: (01604) 21400.

The Society of Teachers of Alexander Technique, 20 London House, 266 Fulham Road, London SW10 9EL. Tel: (0171) 351 0828, e-mail: stat@pavilion.co.uk.

Transcendental Meditation Association, Freepost London SW1P 4YY. Tel: (0990) 143733.

Zero Balancing Association UK, 10 Victoria Grove, Bridport, Dorset DT6 3AA. Tel: (01308) 420007.

Further Reading

Aromatherapy: An A–Z, Patricia Davis (C W Daniel)
Aromatherapy Made Easy, Christine Wildwood (Thorsons)
Feel The Fear and Do It Anyway, Susan Jeffers (Arrow)
Meditation for Inner Peace, Eddie and Debbie Shapiro (Piatkus)
Mind Massage, Marlene Maundril (Capall Bann Publishing)
Super Massage, Gordon Inkeles (Piatkus)
The Self-Help Reflexology Handbook, Sonia Ducie (Vermillion)
Winter Blues, Norman Rosenthal (Guildford Press)
Zero Balancing, John Hamwee

Audio tape
Sleep Better, Feel Better. Details from: Sallyann Sheridan, PO Box 3767, Bridport DT6 6YU. This tape is designed to help sleep come naturally, making you feel better and calmer in your everyday life.

Index